THE HISTORY OF BEARS
ON THE
KODIAK ARCHIPELAGO

by Larry Van Daele

Alaska Natural History Association
Anchorage, Alaska

ACKNOWLEDGMENTS

Although I've been singled out as the sole author of this publication, it is truly a result of the efforts of innumerable people. The impetus behind pulling the various sources of historic information into a single place was the development of a bear management plan in 2000. The plan was sponsored by the Alaska Department of Fish and Game, and was crafted by a Citizens' Advisory Committee. Although the Committee was knowledgeable and resourceful, it was necessary to learn about the past before we planned the future. Interpreting history is somewhat challenging due to varied and sometimes contradictory accounts. Whenever possible, I have relied on written records and cited those records. I've tried to avoid personal recollections and bear stories as much as possible, even though those are often more colorful and interesting than the written records.

This project was funded and supported by the Alaska Department of Fish and Game, Division of Wildlife Conservation. Funding for initial preparation and printing was provided by the Kodiak Brown Bear Trust and New York Tri-State chapter of Safari Club International.

I am especially grateful for the support from several organizations and individuals, who assisted in the development of this monograph. Roger Smith, Ben Ballenger, Vic Barnes, Reed Oswalt, Amy Steffian, and Hilary & Matt Van Daele reviewed and improved several drafts. Nora Deans and Karen Lew provided editorial expertise and ideas on format. Staff from the A. Holmes Johnson public library, the Baranov Museum, the Alutiiq Museum, and the Kodiak National Wildlife Refuge provided a wealth of historic information and photographs. Doris Mensch and John Crye, "covered the office" while I was researching and writing, and they provided moral support, suggestions, and photos.

Tom Walker generously allowed the use of his spectacular photographs of Kodiak bears. Tom also encouraged me to publish this work, and Colleen Matt recommended the Alaska Natural History Association (ANHA) as a source of publication. ANHA, especially Chris Byrd and Patti Harper, has been supportive of the project since its inception. All of the proceeds from the sale of this publication are being returned to ANHA for use in their efforts to educate people about our spectacular natural resources here in Alaska.

Finally, and most importantly, I wish to thank the bruins of the Kodiak islands. Without their patience and understanding for the past 20 years I would never have had the interest or the opportunity to tell the story of how they have learned to share their islands with sometimes unpredictable people.

CONTENTS

INTRODUCTION

INTRODUCTION

Kodiak bears are often portrayed as ferocious beasts, but only one person has been killed by a bear on Kodiak in the past 70 years. About once every other year a bear injures a person.

Kodiak...the name conjures up images of mystery, grandeur, and power. At the heart of that mystique is the mighty Kodiak bear. For thousands of years, people have sought to capture the bear's powerful aura, first in amulets and fetishes, later through the "branding" of all-terrain vehicles and other commercial products.

To guides, hunters, and wildlife photographers, these elusive bears are often viewed as "trophies" and can mean income or prestige. To villagers, sport fishers and deer hunters, the bears are sometimes seen as a nuisance, and a threat. To scientists and wildlife managers, Kodiak bears pose a professional challenge.

The history of how people and bears have survived together on the Kodiak archipelago reflects local, national, and international influences and attitudes. It also embraces the fact that, with understanding and tolerance, people can coexist with a healthy population of the world's largest bears.

The Kodiak Archipelago rises from the sea as part of an uplift zone between two major tectonic plates. Movements between these plates resulted in the first appearance of the islands above the ocean's surface about 30 million years ago, during the Oligocene epoch. Geologic changes continued, and approximately 15 million years ago, during the Miocene epoch, the Kodiak islands reached elevations similar to what we see today (1). Unfortunately, these same geologic forces shifted and changed substrates substantially, and thus a detailed fossil record of the ancient flora and fauna of the islands does not exist. No one knows when bears first arrived on the archipelago.

While Kodiak was rising above the sea, populations of two bearlike animals, the hemicyons and the amphicynodonts, were living throughout Eurasia and North America. The first truly bearlike carnivore probably evolved from one of these animals during the Miocene, giving rise to the "dawn bear" *(Ursavus elmensis)* in Europe (2). Dawn bears spread into North America and eventually gave rise to the ancestor *(Protursus simpsoni)* of today's bear species. The fossil evidence of the genus *Ursus* shows that it first appeared during the Pliocene epoch (five to six million years ago). Direct forerunners of brown bears first appear in the fossil record in China starting approximately 500,000 years ago, and they inhabited much of the Northern Hemisphere by the end of the Pleistocene epoch (12,000 years ago). At that time, brown or grizzly bears *(U. arctos)* and their larger cousins, the short-faced bears *(Arctodus simus)*, both lived in many portions of mainland Alaska and may have made forays to what was to become Kodiak Island.

No one knows when bears first arrived on the archipelago.

Because most of the island was covered by ice sheets extending to the mainland, and sea levels were considerably lower (3), it was also the last opportunity for bears to travel freely between the Kodiak archipelago and the mainland. Soon afterward, the ice receded, inundating the land bridge to the islands. Since then, Kodiak's bears have been genetically isolated, and taxonomists recognize them as a unique subspecies *(U. a. middendorffi)* (4).

Kodiak's habitat at the end of the Pleistocene was considerably different than what is evident today. Bears had less attractive and less abundant food resources because vegetation was recovering from glaciation and salmon runs were just beginning to become established. At that time, the bears were the only large land mammals on the islands, sharing terrestrial areas with red foxes *(Vulpes vulpes)*, river otters *(Lutra canadensis)*, short-tailed weasels *(Mustela erminea)*, little brown bats *(Myotis lucifugus)*, and tundra voles *(Microtus oeconomus)* (5). Humans first arrived on the islands approximately 7,500 years ago, and paleontologic evidence of Kodiak bears is found in some of the oldest midden sites of these ancient Alutiiq people (6). About 3,500 years ago, domestic dogs *(Canis familiaris)* arrived on Kodiak, presumably brought by Alutiiq settlers. Arctic ground squirrels, *(Citellus undulatus)*, were also transplanted to Kodiak and surrounding islands in prehistoric times (7). Sitka spruce *(Picea sitchensis)* invaded the northern islands of the archipelago from the Kenai Peninsula, but did not gain a foothold on the islands until about 800 years ago. By the end of the 1800s, spruce dominated the vegetative overstory of most of Shuyak and Afognak islands, substantially altering fish and wildlife habitats of those areas.

THE FIRST HUMAN INFLUENCE

Early human occupants of the archipelago looked to the sea for their sustenance; most of their activities were along coastal areas with limited use of the interior. Bears (*taquka'aq* in Alutiiq; *medved* in Russian) were seasonally encountered along streams and beaches and were probably attracted to drying fish and garbage pits in settlements. At that time, people occasionally hunted bears, using their meat for food, hides for clothing and bedding, and teeth for adornment. Villagers also used bear intestines for waterproof parkas (*kanaglluk* in Alutiiq; *kamlaika* in Russian) and the long bones for tools. *Kanaglluk* made of bear entrails were considered the strongest, but the material was less plentiful than that obtained from sea lions and seals (8). Bears were usually stalked by groups of two or three hunters armed with bows and arrows. The bear arrow was about 82 cm long and had a barbed bone point 18 cm long with an inserted end blade of slate. If the bear attacked, the hunters defended themselves with spears. Archaeologists speculate that most villages took fewer than three bears per year (9); they also suspect that there were 65 villages and about 8,000 people on the archipelago by the early 1700s.

Fetishes and other artistic renditions of bears occur in archaeological sites on Kodiak dating back 2,500 years. Myths and traditional stories about bears are common in all Alaska Native traditions, and those recorded from Alutiiq Natives are similar to stories still told by Yup'ik elders in western Alaska. The main themes of the myths revolve around the similarity between bears and humans, including the ability of bears to change into people and vice versa, and the mystical nature of bears because of their proximity to the spirit world.

Excavations of early archaeological sites show a notable lack of bear skulls, although other bear bones are present (10a,b). This suggests that bear heads may have been left in the field as a sign of respect to the spirit of the animal, in a ceremony similar to that still practiced today by some Natives in portions of the Alaska Peninsula and western Alaska (11). In more recent archaeological sites, a few bear skulls are present, some of which have the cranium sawed in ways that indicate they were being used for utensils (12).

Male bears are called boars, females are sows, and youngsters are cubs.

Kodiak bears are a unique subspecies of the brown or grizzly bear (*Ursus arctos middendorffi*). They live exclusively on the islands in the Kodiak Archipelago and have been isolated from other bears for about 12,000 years.

COMMERCIAL BEAR HARVEST BY RUSSIANS AND AMERICANS

The Bering expedition "discovered" Kodiak in 1741, and soon thereafter a flood of *promishleniki* (independent trappers) and Russian entrepreneurs came to the area to capitalize on the abundant fur resources. Sea otters (*Enhydra lutris*) possessed the most lucrative pelts, but bears and several other species were also harvested commercially. Between 1796 and 1821, the Russian American

By 1798, when this drawing was made, the Russians were firmly established on Kodiak, monopolizing the sea otter trade and also dealing in bear hides and other furs.

Company exported 2,650 bear hides from the Alaska colonies (an average of 106 bears per year). That number jumped to 5,355 from 1821 through 1842 (an average of 268 per year) as the sea otter harvest declined (13). The price of a bear pelt was comparable to that paid for beaver (*Castor canadensis*) or river otter and about 2 percent of that paid for a sea otter. By the early 1840s, local observations on Kodiak showed a decline in numbers of all kinds of land and amphibious animals, probably caused by the use of firearms in hunting. This prompted the colonial government to prohibit this practice and to discontinue all types of hunting for several years (14). This prohibition was reflected in the Alaska-wide brown bear harvest from 1841 through 1867, when only 2,483 were shipped (an average of 96 per year) (15).

When American military troops were first assigned to Kodiak in 1868, they noted that "brown bears of great size are sometimes killed. The natives eat these when they can get them, but the flesh is rank and disagreeable, as the animal, like the native, lives mostly on fish and shellfish" (16). The troops also observed some Natives using bear hides as kneeling pads in their kayaks. Soon after Seward convinced the United States government to purchase the Alaska Territory from the Russians in 1867, Americans took advantage of their new resources by increasing fur harvests. Brown bear shipments increased to 7,117 between 1867 and 1880 (an average of 548 per year) (17).

Brown bears continued to be harvested commercially until 1925. Fur-shipping records from Alaska between 1912 and 1916 indicate that brown bears were classified as a "minor fur," with an average value of $8.63 per pelt. During the same period, the price of a beaver pelt averaged $10.00, land otter pelts were valued at $9.80, and red fox pelts were valued at $9.03. Kodiak bear pelts were considered in their prime from November 15 through May 31 (18).

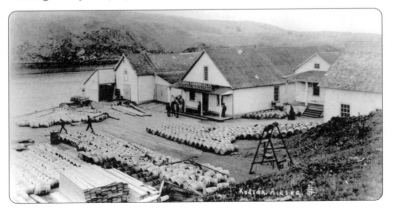

The harvest of bear hides increased substantially after the Americans took possession of the Alaska territory. The Alaska Commercial Company, shown here in the 1900s was the main trading post and fur buyer in Kodiak.

DEVELOPMENT OF COMMERCIAL FISHING

Bear habitat on the Kodiak archipelago remained relatively pristine through the mid-1800s. Human settlements were small, there were no large-scale mining or timber-harvesting operations, and livestock and fishing ventures were limited by unsophisticated preservation technologies. In the early 1800s, Russians adopted the Native stone- and log-dam weirs (*zapruda*) across some salmon-spawning streams, intercepting fish destined for traditional bear-feeding areas. The fish captured at *zaprudas* were dried (*youkala*) for Native hunters to take along on extended sea otter–hunting trips. Sometime near 1827, the Russian American Company prepared 300,000 sockeye salmon (*Oncorhynchus nerka*) per year in this manner (19). They also prepared as many as 600 barrels of salted salmon annually and attempted to market the product, but the commercial ventures were unsuccessful.

By the 1870s, the Americans had taken over the businesses in Kodiak, and the Alaska Commercial Company and the Alaska Fur Trading Company began to market salted salmon on the Pacific coast (20). As did their predecessors, these entrepreneurs had limited success with their commercial fisheries and little impact on the bears. Things changed rapidly in the later part of the century, however, as processors were introduced to economically feasible methods of canning their product.

The first salmon cannery on Kodiak Island was established on the Karluk spit in 1882. The Karluk Packing Company, as the cannery was called, doubled the total output of Alaska canned salmon within its first season, and it was soon joined by numerous competitors on the Karluk and on other important fishing streams on the archipelago. Investors and distributors in the United States were attracted by the seemingly endless supply of high-quality salmon coming from Kodiak, and canneries proliferated.

The first cannery on Kodiak was established on the Karluk spit. By the 1920s, canneries proliferated on the spit and at the mouths of other streams on Kodiak Island and seriously impacted bear feeding opportunities.

On the Karluk River, the annual salmon harvest was about 58,880 in 1882. By 1889, the annual harvest had increased to 3.4 million, with as many as 100,000 salmon caught in a single net (21). Increased competition at the Karluk River enticed fishermen to expand to other streams. Harvest technology became more efficient with longer nets stretched across the rivers and steam power to haul in the larger and heavier nets. Powering of boats evolved from sails to engines, and fishermen learned to set nets and traps in front of river mouths. Markets were developed for all salmon species, and fishing periods were lengthened. In less than a decade, a local enterprise turned into a world-class industry, and the number of salmon available for bears declined sharply.

It soon became apparent that Kodiak's salmon runs could not withstand the intensifying pressure, and legislators feared Kodiak salmon would suffer the fate of the Sacramento River and Columbia River runs. In 1889, the U.S. Congress outlawed the practice of barricading streams so that salmon could not pass. Unfortunately, this law did not have the desired impact, so it was amended in 1896 and 1900 to reduce legal fishing periods to fewer than six days per week and to prohibit the use of nets within 100 yards of stream mouths (22). In 1892, a presidential proclamation established the Afognak Island Forest and Fish Culture Reserve and ordered an immediate halt to commercial and subsistence salmon fishing in the area until a hatchery could be built. Although there were probably positive impacts of the legislation, fisheries agents were hard pressed to enforce these new conservation laws.

Bear conservation was not a deciding factor in preserving salmon resources, but the bears and their habitat undoubtedly benefited from the actions. Unfortunately, however, increased competition for salmon also led to direct persecution of natural predators. Bounties were paid by the federal government for eagles ($0.50–$2.00), and records from the Territorial Legislature indicate that, during the time the program was active (1917-1952), 128,273 eagles were turned in across Alaska (23). Dolly varden were also bountied because they consumed salmon eggs. Bears were not included in this sanctioned predator-control program, but they were routinely shot when seen, and some canneries offered "unofficial" bounties on bears (24). Bears were also targeted by a burgeoning cattle industry that was developing at the same time as were the commercial fisheries.

CATTLE INDUSTRY ORIGINS

Russians brought the first livestock to Kodiak soon after their arrival, and by the late 1790s, cattle, sheep, goats, and pigs were common assets at settlement sites (25). In 1833, the inventory of the Russian American Company alone showed 220 cattle. These cattle provided many Alutiiq people with their first taste of milk and domestic meat, and some bears were also quick to acquire a taste for this new delicacy.

Early historic records are remarkably devoid of references to nuisance bears in villages or to dangerous bear-human encounters. Letters written by the Russian pioneer Grigorii Shelikof to his government in 1786 and 1787 recommended that, in addition to

Russian settlers brought the first livestock to Kodiak in the late 1700s, precipatating a long and troubled relationship between bears and ranchers.

sending livestock to the new colony, "two pairs of ferocious dogs" should also be sent, perhaps as an attempt to deter bear problems. The plan was not without its drawbacks, however, as a Kodiak priest named Archmandrite Ioasaph noted in a 1795 letter to Shelikof: "The dogs have eaten up two of the calves . . . and two of

11

the sheep . . ." (26). In 1878, another Russian official, Ivan Petroff, noted that "a Swede who settled 10 miles out of Kodiak has lost all his cows this year, killed by bear within a few yards of his house" (27).

Cattle numbers varied through the 1800s, but continued to increase. Kodiak's luxuriant grasslands tempted more and more ranchers, and in 1906, the U.S. Department of Agriculture established an experimental station in Kodiak to refine cattle breeds and develop methods to take advantage of the seemingly limitless range. Unfortunately, it was probably the same rapidly growing forage that initially brought cattle and bears together, and thereby expanded the diet of some bears.

While Kodiak provides abundant grazing opportunities in the summer, the grasses and sedges on the island do not hold their nutrient value through the winter. Frequent rains, which make cutting and curing hay very difficult, further challenge ranchers. By late winter and early spring, cattle must obtain supplemental feed from ranchers or face starvation. Those that die during the winter often do so along beaches or other low-elevation areas where they strive to find the last available bits of food. When bears awaken and leave their dens in the spring, most move down to these same areas while seeking the first fresh vegetative growth of the new year. If cattle have died in the area, the bears are rewarded not only with fresh vegetation, but also with tempting beef carcasses.

Though Kodiak bears are often touted as the world's largest land carnivore (meat eaters), they are really omnivores (using a variety of foods). They actually spend more time eating grass, plants and berries than meat. Fish are an important part of their diets, but few Kodiak bears expend the time or effort necessary to chase and kill mammals.

Live cattle will also come into the lowlands and south-facing slopes seeking emerging plants. In their weakened condition, the cattle may become mired in melting bogs or be swept away by avalanches of snow or soil or both as the steep slopes are warmed by the sun. Because of bears' superb adaptability when it comes to finding food, it is easy to see how individual bears could shift from eating vegetation to eating cattle carcasses and eventually shift to killing weakened cattle and calves. Some bears also became adept at facing the daunting task of killing healthy adult cattle, a behavior entirely foreign to their Kodiak ancestors but well within their physical abilities and a common occurrence among their grizzly cousins.

SPORTSMEN INITIATE BEAR CONSERVATION

As the 1800s drew to a close, America was enjoying a period of economic prosperity and optimism. Fueled by the promises of "Manifest Destiny," the nation pushed through the west capitalizing on the abundant resources. Unfortunately, the flora and fauna of the expanding nation did not prove as resilient to abuse as had been imagined. By the late 1880s, the legendary buffalo herds were virtually eliminated, and other wildlife populations were suffering. Sportsmen, who spent much of their time and wealth in pursuit of these animals, were among the first to notice the declines, and they took action to alleviate the problems.

In 1887, the first American wildlife conservation organization was formed when several influential hunters, scientists, and military and political leaders initiated the Boone & Crockett Club (28). Among the precepts of the fledgling organization was "to work for the preservation of the large game of this country and, so far as possible, to further legislation for that purpose and to assist in enforcing existing laws." That was a lofty goal: at the close of the century, the country's game laws were tangled, contradictory, and often unenforceable.

By the 1900s Kodiak bears were recognized as the largest in the world. Big-game hunters noted, however, that the bears had been so hunted that there were too few to ever make shooting them popular, and finding large specimens was increasingly difficult.

Efforts by the Boone & Crockett Club and one of its founders, George Bird Grinnell, led to the first federal legislation to enforce wildlife regulations and the interstate traffic of illegally taken animals. The Game and Wild Bird Preservation and Disposition Act of 1900, also known as the Lacey Act, set the foundation for the first legal protection for much of America's wildlife, including Kodiak's bears. The cause of wildlife conservation was also pushed to the forefront of the nation's consciousness by the first president of the new century, Theodore Roosevelt, another of the Boone & Crockett Club's founders.

In their search for exotic big game trophies and scientific specimens, hunters came to Kodiak to seek what they asserted were the largest bears in the world. In 1896, research done by taxonomist C.H. Merriam confirmed that assertion, and he named the species in honor of the celebrated Russian naturalist Dr. A. Th. von Middendorff (29). Reports and collections from the Harriman Expedition in 1899 furthered Kodiak's reputation. This expedition, financed by business tycoon Edward H. Harriman, brought 25 distinguished American scientists, including Grinnell, on a two-month journey along the Alaska coast. While the journey was billed as a "floating university," one of Harriman's stated objectives for it was to kill a large bear from Kodiak for his trophy room (30).

One of the first detailed accounts of a sportsman's journey to Kodiak was by James H. Kidder (31). He spent several months between March and July 1901 hunting with Native guides from baidarkas. Although he was finally able to collect a large specimen, he noted that "for many years, these bears have been so persistently hunted by the Natives, who are constantly patrolling the shores in their skin canoes, that their [the bears'] knowledge of man and their senses of smell and hearing are developed to an extreme degree." He also stated that "most people have an exaggerated idea of the number of bears on the Kadiak Islands. Personally I believe that they are too few ever to make shooting them popular." (Note: from 1890 to 1901, the island's official name was changed to "Kadiak.") Kidder also noted that Natives throughout the archipelago enjoyed bear meat, but that the pursuit of that delicacy was sometimes fatal to both parties; he heard several stories of Native hunters being killed by injured bears.

The public's interest in Kodiak bears was further piqued by publication of *The King Bear of Kadiak Island* in 1912 (32). Written as part of a series for young men interested in big-game hunting, this novel described in detail the trip from San Francisco to Kodiak, preparations for the hunt, and the hunt itself. Like Kidder's narrative, it warned the potential hunter that it was difficult to find bears on Kodiak and that getting close enough for a kill was even less likely.

MOUNT KATMAI ERUPTION

Kodiak's ecosystem changed rapidly and drastically on June 6, 1912, when Mount Katmai (Novarupta) erupted. A series of three major eruptions blew six cubic miles of the mountain into the air (33). In Kodiak, the eruption caused 60 hours of complete darkness, due to thick ash and sulfurous smoke, punctuated with tremendous electrical storms.

The ashfall and fear of a tsunami prompted evacuation of the entire populace of Kodiak (about 400 people) on the revenue cutter *Manning* (34). Pumice and ash covered the harbor, near-shore waters, and all of the streams and lakes used for drinking water. Most of the ash on the archipelago fell on Afognak and northern Kodiak islands, where it varied in depth from 4 to 12 inches (35). Winds easily drifted the ash, and rains washed it into lakes, completely filling some that were as deep as five feet. Subsequent minor eruptions produced sulfuric fumes potent enough to stain ship hulls near Kodiak and acid rains that irritated eyes (36).

During the ashfall, there were reports of birds falling from the sky. Ptarmigan and small mammals were buried alive, and some salmon-spawning streams were choked with ash. Kelp beds from Katmai to the eastern shore of Afognak Island were killed, as were mussels and barnacles in some areas (37). Residents reported that many animals, including bears, were blinded and made bold by hunger, and bear attacks on cattle near Kodiak increased. Salmon spawning was seriously impacted because the ash pushed fish already in the streams back to sea or killed them in the mud (38). In spite of persistent high turbidity, a few salmon were still able to return during the summer and were available for bears. Salmon returns to the newly established hatchery at Afognak Lake were very low in 1912 and did not rebound until 1917 (39). Vegetation was quicker to recover because grass, lupine, and many shrubs were able to break through the ash by the end of the summer. Local residents credited the ash with increasing productivity of grass, shrubs, and especially spruce in the years following the eruption (40). While the ash probably had a dramatic impact on the bears on the north end of the archipelago, it was not catastrophic for the population as a whole.

In June 1912, Mt. Katmai blew six cubic miles of itself into the air, depositing as much as a foot of ash on Afognak and north Kodiak islands. Vegetation was blanketed, streams and lakes were choked, and small mammals and birds perished. The volcano's explosion had a dramatic impact in some bears, but did not adversely affect the entire population.

THE ALASKA GAME COMMISSION

Professional interest in guided Kodiak bear hunts, and a concern for unregulated resource use in frontier lands such as Alaska, prompted the territorial government's newly established Alaska Game Commission to abolish commercial bear hunting (selling the hides) on the Kodiak archipelago in 1925. A limit of three harvested bears per year was established, and in 1926, bear harvesting was prohibited during the summer months, except for in defense of life or property. At the same time, the Alaska Game Commission, in conjunction with local Kodiak sportsmen's groups, took an active role in enhancing the wildlife diversity of the

Kodiak bears were still prestigious trophies for wealthy hunters from around the world in the 1920s and 1930s and W. Erskine (pictured), his father, and C. Madsen catered to the hunters' needs. In 1928, Madsen became the first registered guide on Kodiak Island.

archipelago. Fourteen deer *(Odocoileus hemionius sitkensis)* were captured in the Sitka area in 1924 and released on Long Island, near the city of Kodiak. Two additional deer, from Prince of Wales Island, were released on Long Island in 1930, and nine more, from Petersburg, were released on Kodiak in 1934 (41). In 1928, eight Roosevelt elk calves *(Cervus elaphus roosevelti)* were imported to Kodiak from the Olympic Peninsula in Washington. These calves spent their first year at the Agricultural Experiment Station at Kalsin Bay, however because of concerns about competition with cattle on Kodiak Island, the elk were released in 1929 near Litnik on Afognak Island (42). Other successful translocations during that period included reindeer at Alitak Bay (1924); muskrat *(Ondata zibethica)* to a variety of locations on northeastern Kodiak, Afognak, Whale, and Spruce islands (1925); beaver to Clark's Lake and Kalsin Bay on Kodiak (1925); and snowshoe hares *(Lepus americanus)* to Kodiak and Afognak islands (1934) (43). While these new denizens probably had little immediate impact on the bear population, the future ramifications would be tremendous.

The popularity of Alaska cruises and collecting trips with wealthy clients increased through the 1920s and into the 1930s, and Kodiak bears continued to be prestigious trophies. Charles Madsen, a local Kodiak merchant and fur trader, hosted and escorted many hunters throughout this period. In 1925, the Alaska Game Commission required that any nonresident hunter in Alaska be accompanied in the field by a registered big-game guide. Madsen pursued the guiding requirements, and, in 1928, he became the first registered guide in Kodiak, establishing the Kodiak Guiding Association. His full-time guiding business included camps at Karluk Lake and the east arm of Uganik Bay (Mush Bay).

STEER WARS—EPISODE ONE

While Americans were enjoying the "Roaring Twenties" and struggling through the economic challenges of the 1930s, big game

Afognak Island was set aside as the first forerunner of a National Wildlife Refuge in 1892. From 1932-1940 it was also a bear sanctuary and all bear hunting was prohibited.

guides and their clients were pursuing agenda for the bear population that were remarkably different from the desires of Kodiak cattlemen. The competing interests are evident in the evolution of bear-hunting regulations in that period. In 1928, the bag limit was reduced to two bears per year; in 1929, however, the commission protected cattlemen on the archipelago by stipulating that ". . . on Kodiak, Afognak, Raspberry, Spruce, and Sitkalidak islands, a resident engaged in agricultural pursuits may kill a large brown or grizzly bear at any time or place when such animal is considered a menace to persons, livestock, or property" (44). This caveat failed to satisfy many local residents, and, in 1930, there was again no closed season and an unlimited bag limit for resident bear hunters on all of the archipelago except Shuyak. In 1931, the Karluk, Sturgeon, and Uyak Bay drainages joined Shuyak in having restricted seasons (September 1-June 20) and bag limits (two bears per year) for all bear hunters. The unrestricted resident bear hunting on Kodiak ended in 1933 when it, too, was included within the season and bag limits for the other parts of the islands.

In 1932, the Game Commission closed all bear hunting on Afognak Island, noting that "because of the importance of the Afognak Island Reservation, which was established by Executive Proclamation in 1892 as a sanctuary for wild animals and birds as well as fish, attention is directed to its value for the preservation of the exceedingly interesting Kodiak bear by including it in the areas named in regulation 14, by which all hunting of this bear is prohibited" (45). This area remained closed to bear hunting until 1940. Also in 1932, the commission mandated that nonresident bear photographers could not "pursue or disturb a large brown or grizzly bear" unless accompanied by a registered big game guide.

The impacts of eliminating the commercial harvest of bears and of the sport harvest restrictions had a dramatic effect on populations of bears on the Kodiak islands. W.J. Erskine, proprietor of the trading station that had previously been owned by the Alaska Commercial Company, noted that, during the peak of the commercial harvest, as many as 250 hides were handled annually, but that, by 1937, the overall harvest had dwindled to about 12 per year, most taken by big game hunters (46). There were also a few cubs captured under permit for zoological parks. Erskine and guide Charles Madsen noted a substantial increase in bear numbers in their hunting area at Uganik Bay during the 1930s. Erskine estimated the bear population on Kodiak at 5,000 bears, while Madsen estimated 3,000 (47). A petition to the Alaska Game Commission by Kodiak cattle ranchers in May 1937 stated that "it is estimated, here, by people competent to do so, that there are about five times the number of bear on Kodiak Island than there were before the law, protecting these predatory animals, was passed . . . ."

Ranchers and other Kodiak residents demanded action to reduce bear problems, and the Game Commission sent a biologist to the island to investigate. L.J. Palmer spent three weeks on Kodiak Island and concluded that ". . . due to being protected and little hunted, the bear have so increased that they are more and more invading all parts of the Island. The general increase and invasion is such as to have resulted in depredations to white settlement and aroused the present complaints not only by livestock owners, but by cannerymen and fishermen as well." Palmer recommended a dividing line be drawn from Viekoda Bay to Kiliuda Bay on Kodiak. Lands to the south and west of this line were to be

Elimination of commercial bear hunting in 1925 significantly reduced the bear harvest on Kodiak. By 1937, sport hunters were only taking about a dozen bears annually, with several more killed for museum specimens and some cubs captured for zoos.

considered bear country. East of the line was cattle country, and bears, particularly the "stock killers," would be hunted to reduce their numbers. He further recommended that one experienced predator hunter and at least two local assistants be employed for this task (48).

In March 1939, the Secretary of Agriculture issued a permit allowing the Alaska Game Commission to kill as many as 25 adult brown bears in the cattle country of northeastern Kodiak Island. Later that month, a wildlife agent, accompanied by two professional bear hunters, came to Kodiak and remained through the summer with the expressed purpose to ". . . make all efforts to take any and all bears seen in the proximity of any cattle range with intentions of reducing their numbers within the cattle area, as well as removing them whenever possible as a potential menace in the neighborhood of livestock" (49). The agent and the hunters also spent considerable time interviewing Kodiak residents and investigating all known cattle losses. In the end, they saw 16 bears and were able to kill seven. They recorded 113 cattle losses, of which only three were confirmed bear kills. Late-winter mortality (starvation) and accidents were the primary causes of cattle deaths.

Although some of the cattlemen confided that losses to bears were not as great as losses to other factors, they strongly believed that bear reduction or elimination, through bounties or direct government intervention, was the only factor they could control to improve their industry. Game Commission agents noted that these beliefs had ". . . caused them [the cattlemen] to develop a bitter hatred for the bear that has grown into an obsession. They have shouted their hatred to the world, and their friends and sympathizers have, with more enthusiasm and sympathy than direct knowledge and good judgment, taken up the cry and broadcast it far and wide. Exaggeration has been their strongest point. . . . It is little wonder that many of the people in the vicinity of the cattle area clamor for a price upon his head and are afraid to go outside after dark for a bucket of water" (50). In conclusion, the agents discouraged the idea of further bear-control efforts and the concept of dividing the island into cattle country and bear country. They encouraged managing the island primarily for "fur, fish, and game" resources, including bears, and continuing to allow individuals to defend their livestock. They also requested that the government be more active in disseminating factual information on the numerous perils of raising livestock on Kodiak Island. As a consequence of that report, the Game Commission did not liberalize bear hunting regulations nor did it pursue any further active bear control.

THE REFUGE AND WORLD WAR II

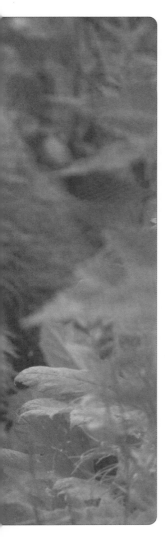

As the nation and the world slid steadily toward one of the largest global conflicts ever known to man, the United States government forged two important pieces of legislation that had profound impacts on the future of bears on Kodiak. In 1937, the Federal Aid in Wildlife Restoration Act, better known as the Pittman-Robertson Act, provided a secure source of funding for state wildlife management and habitat acquisition programs. The source of this funding was an excise tax levied on the sale of firearms and ammunition. Prior to receiving any of these funds, states had to prove that their programs were "substantial in character and design" and that all revenues from hunting licenses would be used to fund wildlife programs (51). Although Alaska was not to become a state for another 22 years, this act set the stage for developing and funding the Alaska Department of Fish and Game.

The other federal action, which had a more immediate and direct impact on the bears, was Executive Order 8857, which created the Kodiak National Wildlife Refuge. When President Franklin D. Roosevelt signed this order on August 19, 1941, he withdrew 1,957,000 acres from unreserved public domain to preserve the natural feeding and breeding range of the brown bear and other wildlife. The area encompassed all of Uganik Island and most of the southwestern portion of Kodiak Island, except for the 35,200-acre Karluk Indian Reservation (established in 1942 by Public Land Order 128). A one-mile shoreline strip remained open for public entry (52).

World War II brought an unprecedented increase of people, structures, and activity to Alaska. The population of Kodiak city swelled from about 400 to more than 20,000 in a few years (53). A submarine base, an air station, a fleet weather command, and an army command post were established near the Buskin River. Remote submarine and aircraft observation posts were developed on numerous islands and capes in the archipelago. On Afognak Island, the U.S. Army developed logging operations at Kazakof (Danger) Bay and near the head of Afognak Bay. The U.S. Navy built an amphibious aircraft base on Afognak Lake.

In 1942, Public Land Order 71 withdrew from the refuge 7,650 acres near Lazy Bay for an enemy aircraft surveillance site, with the stipulation that lands revert back to refuge status when no longer needed for military purposes. Although sport hunting for bears declined during the war years, indirect impacts on the bears abounded, and, in 1942, the Game Commission provided the bears further protection by reducing the bag limit on the archipelago to one bear per year.

BEAR-SALMON CONFLICTS

Refuge establishment and the war did little to quell the concerns about bears preying on salmon. During the first 10 years' (1921–1930) operation of the Karluk River weir, the mean annual escapement was 1.2 million sockeye salmon. By the mid-1940s, the average escapement had dwindled to 0.4 million. Fishermen and some biologists were quick to target bears as a leading cause of this decline, noting that "on several of the small streams, it was found that the bear were destroying every salmon entering to spawn" (54). They suggested that bear populations had increased during the war years because of the decrease in hunting pressure and movement of bears away from military installations and into remote areas such as the Karluk drainage.

The first objective investigation of this problem occurred in 1947. During that study, biologists estimated that bears killed 31 percent of the salmon entering the Karluk River system before they had a chance to spawn. Shuman (55) estimated the financial loss to the territory at $3 million and called for immediate action: ". . . the existing bear population in the Karluk area is inimical to the survival of the sockeye runs, and the existence of a valuable resource is being threatened. Elimination or extermination of the bear need not and should not be attempted, but a control of the population is needed urgently. Suitable measures which will bring the population to a reasonable level should be instituted without delay".

Fisheries observers began estimating bear numbers and population trends around Karluk Lake in 1952; in 1953, biologists estimated the percentage of unspawned salmon taken by bears in selected Karluk tributaries (56). During that same year, refuge staff also produced the first management plan for Kodiak bears (57). That plan described several attempts to keep bears away from salmon spawning streams, including setting air-raid sirens to sound every five minutes, lobbing dummy grenades at feeding bears, and bombing bears along the Karluk River from aircraft. The only deterrence method that showed promise was erection of electric fences around small tributary streams. The plan also suggested dividing Kodiak Island into nine bear management districts and limiting harvest of the estimated 1,669 bears on the island to a maximum of 204 annually (58).

In 1954, Kodiak National Wildlife Refuge staff inaugurated a study designed to investigate bear-salmon interactions. They employed a variety of methods to estimate bear numbers, diet, movements and the impacts of bears on spawning salmon (59). The biologists estimated that the Karluk bear population was stable at approximately 1.5 bears per square mile. Diets varied seasonally, including primarily alpine vegetation in July, salmon in August, and elderberry in September. Interestingly, this study revealed that bears had little impact on salmon spawning. Clark (60) noted that, on Halfway Creek, bears took about 25 percent of the fish that entered the stream, but only 1.5 percent of the unspawned salmon. These results were the same as those noted by Grogen two years earlier. Clark attributed this low use of unspawned salmon to rapid egg deposition and fertilization once the salmon reached the spawning grounds. Within 24 hours of reaching the stream, most female salmon had dug redds and deposited more than 50 percent of their eggs. He also noted that "bear have little chance to take wholly unspawned salmon in small streams because of their return to safety of the lake on molestation during ascension" and that "grazing and use of berries account for probably three-fourths of the yearly diet" (61).

Bear hunters and conservationists strongly opposed the concept of bear control, and they voiced their opinions in the popular press nationwide. In 1951, *Field and Stream* magazine included a description of the impact of Shuman's report (62) when it was presented by commercial fishing and cattlemen's groups at the Alaska Game Commission meeting. The commission reportedly was not swayed when "the largest bears on the planet had been weighed against cases of canned salmon and [were] found wanting" (63). In a *Field and*

Bears had little impact on salmon spawning.

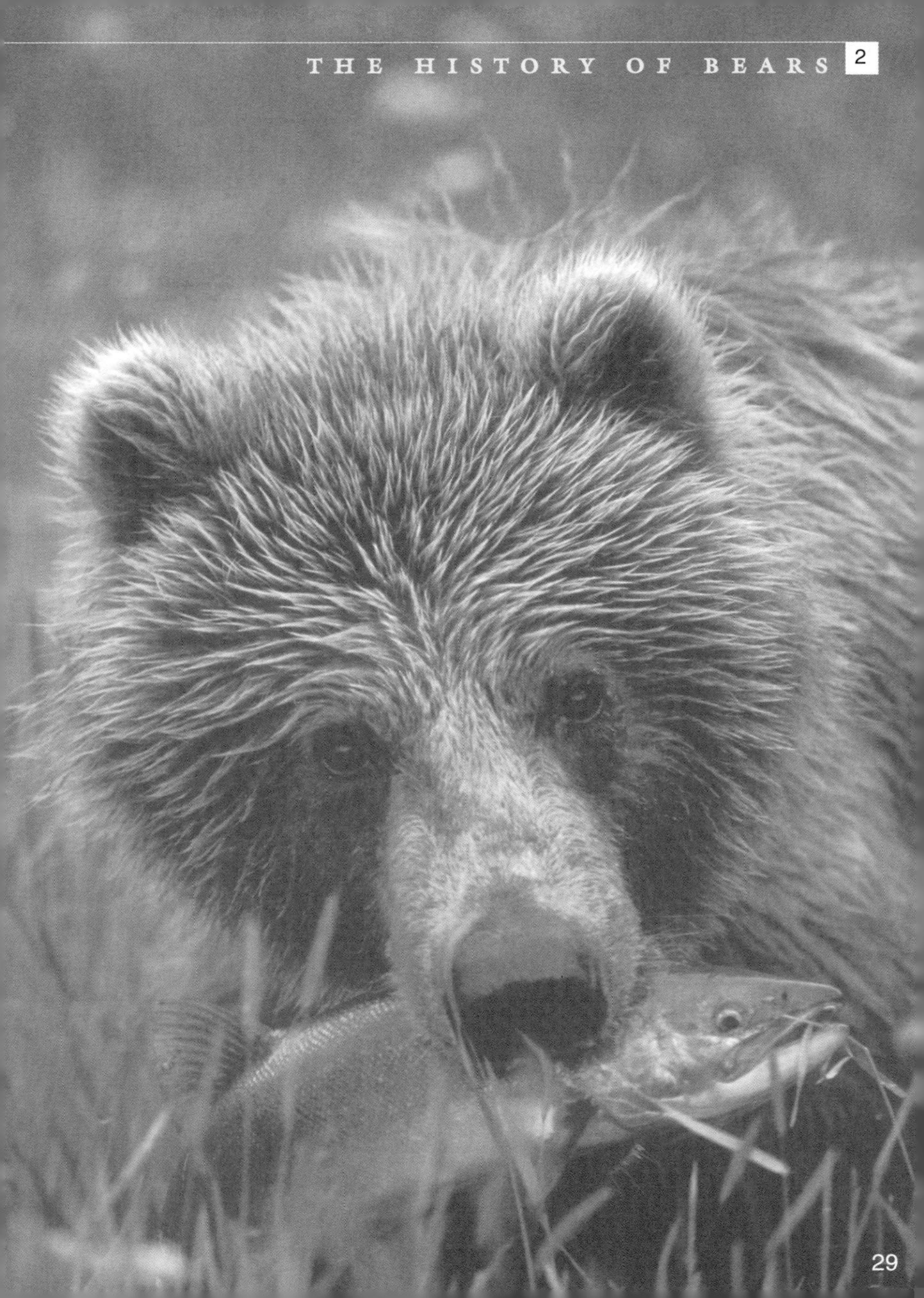

Stream article two years later, another author said, "Conservationists and sportsmen all over America, aroused by the Kodiak threat, have joined battle in the bear's defense" (64). An article in the *Saturday Evening Post* in 1955 noted "unless the species is given continued protection, the conservationists warn, America's most majestic wildlife creature could be wiped out in a few short years. The trouble is . . . that the big bears don't have a lobby in Washington. Surely a nation as big as ours can afford a few acres of real estate . . . so that this historic creature will not go the way of

Killing females accompanied by cubs was outlawed in 1957, but some unscrupulous hunters found a loophole in the regulation by killing the cubs first and then killing the sow. In 1958, the law was amended to also protect cubs.

the mastodon and the hairy mammoth, and disappear from the face of the earth" (65).

At the same time, writers were questioning the ferocity of Kodiak bears. Most authors glamorized the bears as a "prehistoric monster with cleavers for claws and a head the size of an over-turned shovel scoop; the paralyzing glimpse of ears laid back and fangs bared and white with foam slobbering from its jaws, the sound of ear-splitting rage—are enough to deduct at least a decade from your allotted life span" (66). These descriptions were quick to catch the attention of readers, but had little basis in fact, as many writers later pointed out. One popular article, written by a seasonal employee of the Kodiak National Wildlife Refuge, sought to counter these depictions of bear behavior by describing his encounters with more than 400 brown bears, 80 of which approached him. He reported that brown bears are not interested in injuring people and would rather retreat than challenge humans (67).

After considering these diverse opinions and the results of the biological investigations, together with the concerns of fishermen and continued concerns about bear-cattle interactions, the Alaska Game Commission again opted to forego any bear control or hunting-season liberalization. It did, however, pass a new regulation in 1957 that protected maternal female bears statewide. The next year, that protection was extended to also include dependent cubs. The U.S. Department of the Interior also took action to alleviate bear-cattle conflicts when the Secretary of the Interior closed a one-mile strip around the Kodiak National Wildlife Refuge to public entry on May 9, 1958 (Public Land Order 1634). This action was based on a review of the original purpose of the one-mile strip (homesteads and cannery operations) and an analysis of the suitability of the area for grazing. Refuge staff concluded that ". . . grazing activities that included all or a portion of the one-mile strip . . . would result in increased pressure for the reduction of Brown Bear and consequently be detrimental of the conservation of this animal in the Refuge area" (68). In exchange, the refuge forfeited the Shearwater and Kupreanof peninsulas, opening them as unreserved public domain. This reduced the size of the refuge by more than 130,000 acres, but it effectively separated grazing lands from refuge lands and curtailed land disposals and cabin development along the coastal fringe of the refuge.

BIOLOGICAL RESEARCH AND STATE MANAGEMENT

In 1957, refuge biologists made their first attempts at capturing bears with culvert traps located at Thumb and O'Malley creeks.

Although bear research efforts started off slowly, by the early 1960s, U.S. Fish and Wildlife Service biologists had developed methods to capture, mark, and follow bears on Kodiak Island.

Their efforts were more a learning experience than an unmitigated success, but two bears were caught (one was caught twice) and marked with "cattle-type" ear tags (69). The most significant aspect of these continuing investigations was recognition of a declining bear population in the area.

Bear seasons and bag limits changed little during the 1940s and 1950s, with seasons remaining open from September through the end of May. There was, however, an increasing interest in Kodiak bear hunting following the war years. Alaska in general, and Kodiak in particular, was revealed to a multitude of Americans during the war, and postwar prosperity made the trip north more affordable to many hunters. The island also became easier to access because of the construction of the Kodiak airport in 1939 and commencement of commercial air service soon thereafter. The Navy base continued to operate after the war ended, bringing a regular rotation of young hunters anxious to test their abilities on the world-famous Kodiak bear. Hunting and fishing were excellent ways to maintain morale for Navy personnel, and numerous opportunities were provided by the base, including conversion of the hatchery on Afognak Lake to a naval recreational facility.

Biologists began monitoring bear harvests in 1950 by employing a mandatory export permit system on the Kodiak National Wildlife Refuge and field checks throughout the archipelago. They noted increasing harvests along Karluk Lake and the bays on northern and western Kodiak Island (70a-b), but had few tools to measure the impact of those harvests on the bear population. To address the research and management deficiencies, the Kodiak National Wildlife Refuge staff and the newly established State of Alaska focused efforts on understanding and conserving Kodiak bears. Refuge biologists shifted the emphasis of their research on Karluk Lake from salmon depredation (71) to gathering baseline biological information on bears (72). As they refined methods of capturing and marking bears (73) and incorporating radio telemetry in 1967 (74), biologists became more efficient at estimating bear movements and density. Their studies also provided the first objective data on sex and age ratios (75), reproduction (76a-c), litter sizes, behavior (77), cannibalism (78), dentition (79), and denning (80).

On January 3, 1959, Alaska became the 49th state and soon thereafter, the Alaska Department of Fish and Game assumed responsibility for managing the state's wildlife resources. The department was charged with ensuring that the wildlife ". . . belonging to the state shall be utilized, developed, and maintained on the sustained yield principle, subject to preferences among beneficial uses" (Section 4, Alaska State Constitution). To achieve this goal on Kodiak, the fledgling state agency and the Alaska Game Commission's successor, the Alaska Board of Game, reduced bear hunting seasons on Afognak and Raspberry islands and on the Kodiak National Wildlife Refuge. They also implemented a hide-sealing requirement, established a tag fee for nonresident bear hunters, and stationed a game biologist in Kodiak. However, the new state's constitution further stated that "the legislature may provide for facilities, improvements, and services to assure greater utilization, development, reclamation, and settlement of lands . . ." (Section 5). The state addressed this mandate by liberalizing bear seasons on nonrefuge lands on Kodiak Island and by initiating another official investigation into the bears on northeastern Kodiak that had developed a taste for beef.

STEER WARS—THE SEQUEL

From May 1964 through June 1965, Alaska Department of Fish and Game biologists worked with ranchers along the Kodiak road system to determine the extent of the predation problem, the sex and age composition of the bear population in the area, and the origin and movement patterns of bears in the area (81). They also actively pursued and killed all bears suspected to be cattle killers. During the study, bears killed 33 cattle, and 19 bears were killed (four by hunters and the remainder as predators). Most of the cattle were killed in the spring, and all of the predator bears that were killed were adult males. The study concluded that "Kodiak brown bears are an effective predator on cattle and [cattle and] bears are not compatible on the same ranges" (82). Potential solutions included poisons distributed by department personnel, erection of a chain-link fence (8-10 feet high) from Kizhuyak Bay to Hidden Basin to isolate cattle ranges from bear areas, and working with land managers to prevent further land disposals that would exacerbate competition between bears and cattle (83).

Efforts to further the idea of fencing continued through 1966, with some material purchased, bids offered, and several sites examined, including the original Kizhuyak-to-Hidden Basin route, a route from Middle Bay to Saltery Cove, and additional routes to isolate Kupreanof and Shearwater peninsulas. Cost estimates ranged as high as $750,000, and Senator Barry Goldwater from Arizona was reportedly prepared to seek federal funding for the project. Guides and ranchers favored the fencing project; in the end, however, it was decided that an extensive bear fence was not feasible, and the concept was eventually dropped. Active involvement in killing predatory bears proved to be a more enduring activity.

As happened with the bear-salmon and bear-cattle conflicts in the early 1950s, sportsmen did not hesitate to make their voices heard in support of Kodiak brown bears. The most vociferous condemnation of the predator-control program came in an article in *Outdoor Life* titled "The Kodiak Bear War" (84). A group of Kodiak guides sent a telegram to the editor requesting that the magazine present the facts to the public. In its exposé, the magazine disclosed a "secret" state-sanctioned program that started in 1962 and employed the use of two World War II fighter pilots to shoot bears from the air. The Piper Super Cub aircraft with a semi-automatic M-1 Garand rifle mounted above the cockpit was prominently displayed on the magazine's cover. There were also detailed descriptions of the ground efforts by biologists and the ongoing anti-bear campaign by ranchers. In a response to a letter from the Alaska Ornithological Society about the predator-control program, the director of Alaska Department of Fish and Game's Game Division wrote, "This problem on Kodiak is placing the Department of Fish and Game in the difficult position of extending protection to cattle ranchers while safeguarding the bears. Obviously, these two responsibilities are inimical, and it is difficult to reassure all groups that our handling of the problem reflects a realistic weighing of contrary interests" (85).

The department continued its involvement in dispatching problem bears and attempted to capture and move some bears. According to Alaska Department of Fish and Game records, from 1966 through 1969, the Board of Game also authorized the use of dogs to pursue and hunt brown bears on northeastern Kodiak. In spite of these official actions, ranchers became frustrated with the inefficiency of the biologists' attempts to minimize the number of cattle killed by bears. Several ranchers became more aggressive in their efforts to remove bears by baiting, snaring, and poisoning, usually failing to salvage or report their kills. In one case, a bear that had been darted by a biologist was shot and killed by an "informed but uncooperative" ranch hand before the helicopter could land to translocate the bear out of the Saltery Lake area. In 1969, the area game biologist expressed his concern that 10 percent of the reported Unit 8 (Kodiak Archipelago) bear harvest was attributed to control programs. In a memorandum to his supervisor, he noted that "department involvement in a predator-control program on brown bears is undesirable from the game management viewpoint" (86).

In November 1970, the department reevaluated its role in bear management on Kodiak, and the director of the Game Division wrote (87):

> The following shall be the Department's policy concerning predation of cattle by brown bear:
> - The Department shall not participate in brown bear depredation programs designed to alleviate cattle losses.

35¢ · AUGUST, 1964

Outdoor Life

MOST DANGEROUS GAME
No. 3: The Leopard

N.Y. SUBWAY FISHING
Hudson River Bonanza

THE ALLAGASH STORY

**ALSO: Trout, Salmon,
Deer, Moose, Sheep**

KODIAK BEAR WAR
Killings with M1 Rifle on
Aircraft Arouse Sportsmen

HOW TO FISH WEEDS
For Bass, Pike, Muskies

State biologists assisted ranchers between 1962 and 1969 by actively pursuing and killing suspected predator bears on cattle leases near Kodiak. This enraged guides and other sportsmen, and they took their case to a nationwide audience.In 1970, the Alaska Department of Fish and Game curtailed the predator-control program. A new policy established sport hunting and existing defense of life or property provisions as the only legal means of bear control, and it specifically prohibited shooting from aircraft and the use of poisons for bear control.

- The person suffering these losses may take bears in defense of life or property . . . . Under no circumstances may bear be shot from airplanes or taken by means of any poisonous substance.
- That section of the regulations pertaining to immediate notification of the Alaska Department of Fish and Game upon taking a bear and to written documentation and salvaging of the hide will be strictly enforced.
- The Department will make every effort to keep sport hunting regulations liberal to make possible the effective removal of brown bears by hunters.

This policy reiterated decisions made 30 years earlier by the Alaska Game Commission and appeared to close a long chapter in the relationship among cattlemen, government agents, and Kodiak bears. Ranchers were understandably upset with the decision, however, and they continued to devise creative ways to protect their livestock without government intervention (88).

INCREASING HARVESTS AND CHANGING HABITAT

In the late 1960s, bear hunting regulations for areas not impacted by the predator-control program became progressively stricter in response to increasing hunting pressure. Annual reported sport harvest increased each year from 1961 (97 bears killed) through 1966 (206 bears killed). Same-day airborne hunting was prohibited in 1967. In that same year, hunters were required to bring the skulls of harvested bears out of the field, and, in 1968, skull sealing was required.

Population studies around Karluk Lake suggested the local harvest exceeded the maximum sustainable yield, so the Karluk Lake drainage was closed to fall bear hunting by emergency regulation in 1967 and by regulation in 1968. This closure received national exposure when the King of Nepal allegedly shot a bear within the closed area during a State Department–sanctioned guided hunt in November 1967, according to Alaska Department of Fish and Game files. In an additional effort to better distribute bear harvests on the refuge, Kodiak National Wildlife Refuge staff also imposed a permit quota system in 1968. In 1969, the bag limit for brown bears was reduced from one bear per year to one bear per four years, and the winter hunting season was eliminated for most of the archipelago.

While biologists were actively involved in capturing, killing, and managing bears throughout the 1960s, Kodiak's bruins also experienced some changes in their habitat. In 1962, a fish pass was completed around the falls on Dog Salmon River. The pass allowed returning sockeye salmon access to the rich, virgin, spawning and rearing habitat of Frazer Lake. Since 1951, mature sockeye and eyed eggs had been transported to the lake by air-craft and packboard in an attempt to establish a viable population, but it wasn't until construction of the pass that the run established itself. By 1966, more than 10,000 fish were returning to the lake, providing additional summer feeding opportunities to bears in the area (89).

On March 27, 1964, the entire archipelago shook for as long as seven minutes in what was the most violent earthquake in the recorded history of the state. Most of the islands subsided 5–6 feet, drastically altering the habitat of many lagoons, near shore lakes, and on tide flats. The resulting tsunamis inundated shorelines with run-up heights varying from 5 to 31.5 feet above mean high water (90). Presumably, some bears were killed when their dens collapsed or when they were caught in avalanches precipitated by the earthquake, and some were forced to seek alternate spring food sources to replace those affected by the tsunamis. Overall, however, the bear population did not appear to suffer substantial ill effects from the tremblor.

OIL AND ANSCA

Geologic phenomena on the other side of Alaska, and sociopolitical movements on the other side of the continent, shook the political landscape of the state and nation through the late 1960s and early 1970s and ultimately impacted the brown bear habitat on Kodiak. Natural oil seeps and ponds had been used by Inupiat residents of northern Alaska for centuries. Although several explorers noted these and other oil deposits in the state, it was not until 1898 that shallow wells were developed. After Congress passed the Mineral Leasing Act in 1920, oil exploration expanded throughout the Gulf of Alaska, Cook Inlet, and the north slope of the Brooks Range. In 1923, a presidential order set aside the Naval Petroleum Reserve, and, in 1944, the U.S. Navy instituted an intensive search for new oil reserves (91).

The first large commercial oil field in the state was discovered near the Swanson River on the Kenai Peninsula in 1957; in the same year, more lands on the north slope were opened to leasing. Additional oil and gas fields were discovered in the Cook Inlet region in the 1960s, but it was the discovery of the massive deposit near Prudhoe Bay in December 1967 that thrust Alaska into the limelight as a world-class oil producer. The excitement of the discovery was somewhat tempered, however, by the logistical challenges of recovering the estimated 9.6 billion barrels of high quality crude from the frozen arctic and delivering it to an ice-free port and ultimately to the refineries and consumers concentrated in the contiguous United States. The preferred method of transport was an oil pipeline from Prudhoe Bay to Valdez, which would stretch almost 800 miles and cross lands claimed by the federal and state governments and by several groups of indigenous people.

Concurrent with discovery of oil in Alaska, the United States was experiencing a period of social upheaval and introspection. The escalating conflict in Vietnam was spawning civil unrest and a financial drain. African Americans were continuing their struggle for equal rights, and movements espousing women's rights escalated. Native Americans, including many in Alaska, were seeking equality and restitution for lands and resources they believed had been illegally taken from their ancestors. There was also a rising tide of environmental awareness, which resulted in myriad legislation, including the Wilderness Act (1964), the Clean Water Restoration Act (1966), the Endangered Species acts (1966, 1969, and 1973), the Clean Air Act (1970), the National Environmental Policy Act (1970), and the Marine Mammals Protection Act (1972).

Entrepreneurs and politicians faced this rapidly evolving political climate as they tried to develop and market the oil from the Prudhoe Bay discovery. Pressure to resolve Native land claims escalated in late 1969 when oil companies paid the state more than $900 million for the right to drill for petroleum on the "North Slope." After considerable debate and compromise, the Alaska Native Claims Settlement Act (ANCSA) (Public Law 92-203) was signed into law on December 18, 1971. The new law extinguished aboriginal claims to most of Alaska in exchange for 43.7 million acres of land and $962.5 million. It also included terms in Section 17(d)(2) that provided for setting aside as much as 80 million acres of unreserved federal lands for designation as national parks, national forests, national wildlife refuges, and national wild and scenic rivers.

Petroleum companies explored the Alaska Peninsula and Shelikof Straits and found some promising prospects, but no commercial oil developments were established on or near Kodiak Island. The impacts of ANCSA, however, were felt strongly on the archipelago. Local Native groups selected, as their share of land under ANCSA, virtually the entire coastline of Kodiak as well as the Karluk River drainage; Sitkalidak, Sitkinak, Shuyak, Spruce and Whale islands; much of Uganik Island; and most of the forested areas of Afognak and Raspberry islands. Ultimately, most of these selections—with the exception of Shuyak, Sitkinak, and Uganik islands—were conveyed to the Native corporations. Federal management of the national forest lands on Afognak was threatened, and the Kodiak National Wildlife Refuge lost control of 310,000 acres of prime bear habitat (more than 17 percent of refuge lands). Predictably, the land selections and conveyances were controversial. Local newspaper articles predicted the demise of the bear population as new land managers sought to maximize profits by dramatically expanding cattle grazing operations, establishing lodges on bear feeding streams, harvesting timber, and eventually selling lands to outside interests. Refuge staff also expressed concerns about the potential impacts of ANCSA, but chose to look on the bright side, noting that ". . . the act [ANCSA] awards the federal government the right of first refusal if any of the selected land is ever sold by the village corporation" (92). They also were encouraged by the provisions of the act that stipulated that lands that were previously in the refuge ". . . remain subject to the laws and regulations governing use and development of such refuge" (ANCSA Section 22[g]).

HUNTER MANAGEMENT AND INCREASING COMPLEXITIES

The refuge's bear hunting permit system, initiated in 1968, was initially successful in improving hunter distribution and improving the quality of the hunters' experiences. Many were pleased with the system, which divided the refuge into as many as 75 different hunt units and allowed only one party to be assigned to a unit at a time. There was no limit to the number of people allowed per party, and guides and hunters could pick up permits by proxy. As the program continued, however, it became apparent that there was room for improvement. Guides monopolized many of the most productive times and hunt units for their clients, while some of the more inaccessible units were not used at all. Some hunters moved to units outside of their assigned areas and misrepresented kill locations. In spite of the permit system, eventually most of the harvest was again concentrated in the Karluk Lake and Uyak Bay areas.

Demand for permits increased sharply in 1972 and again in 1973. Restrictions in season length on the Alaska Peninsula and the loss of polar bear hunting after passage of the Marine Mammals Protection Act were partially responsible for the surge in resident hunter and guide interest in Kodiak. Competition for Kodiak permits became keen, and guides began queuing a week or more in advance of the permit issuance date. Most resident hunters had neither the time nor the financial resources to pursue this method effectively, and their chances to hunt prime areas diminished significantly. Increased competition disturbed both the residents and the established Kodiak guides, and they lobbied

Today, hunters kill about 160 Kodiak bears each year under tightly controlled regulations.

for change. Refuge staff sought to rectify the problem by proposing to issue half of the permits to residents and half to nonresidents, but federal solicitors declared this discriminatory and suggested that the only legal method would be a lottery system of permit distribution (93).

In 1975, the state created 19 exclusive guiding areas on the Kodiak archipelago and distributed those areas to long-established guides having historic use and financial investments within the areas. This action eliminated many of the newcomers from the lucrative Kodiak bear hunting market and was touted as a conservation measure that would encourage guides to nurture the resources in their areas. During the same year, the U.S. Fish and Wildlife Service imposed a limit on the number of permits it issued for bear hunting on the refuge. The new permit system did not address concerns about the inequity between resident and nonresident hunting opportunities.

The state government viewed the imposition of limited bear-hunting permits as an affront to the long recognized authority of a state to manage its resident wildlife populations; thus, the state challenged the Service's action and developed a concurrent state permit system. During the fall 1975 season, hunters within refuge boundaries were required to have both state and federal permits. The federal solicitor soon ruled in favor of the state system, and the federal program was dropped. The Alaska Board of Game worked with the Alaska Department of Fish and Game to devise a system in which permits on most of Kodiak Island were distributed by lottery. Drawings were held for both spring and fall hunts, and Alaska residents were allocated at least 60 percent of the permits. Twenty-six hunt areas were established, coinciding as much as possible with the exclusive guide areas, and permit allocation was based on historic harvest patterns, except in overharvested areas. Northeastern Kodiak and the northern islands were not included in the drawing hunt area. To ensure timely and accurate harvest reporting, the new regulations also stipulated that, before they could

be exported from the island, all bears killed on the Kodiak archipelago had to be inspected and sealed by an Alaska Department of
Fish and Game representative in Kodiak.

The guides and the U.S. Fish and Wildlife Service were invited
to participate in drafting the plan, and they were in agreement with
it when it was implemented in time for the Fall 1976 hunting season.
The increased level of cooperation and the enhanced management
options resulted in a permit system that was finally effective in equi-
tably distributing and regulating bear harvests. The discussions also
spawned a cooperative agreement between the Alaska Department
of Fish and Game and the Kodiak National Wildlife Refuge that
outlined their respective roles in managing brown bears and their
habitat on the refuge and agreeing that both parties would meet at
least once a year to evaluate the effectiveness of the permit system.

CHANGING RELATIONSHIPS AND A MANAGEMENT PLAN

While the nation celebrated its bicentennial, relationships
between people and Kodiak bears were changing and becoming
more complicated. Old battles between bears and cattlemen were
at a lull because many of the established ranchers were reducing or
curtailing their operations and few new ones were coming on the
scene. Fishermen had little incentive to be concerned about bear
predation because salmon runs around the islands were increasing
and several fisheries were being established or enhanced. Bear

In the 1970s, bear-human relationships were changing as salmon
and cattle conflicts waned, and hunting and bear viewing demand
increased. To address these demands, the Alaska Department of
Fish and Game proposed a bear-management plan that would have
continued liberalized hunting near the city of Kodiak and the cattle
ranches, encouraged bear viewing at Karluk and Portage lakes, and
managed for high-quality, bear-hunting opportunities on most of the
archipelago. The plan was, however, never formally adopted.

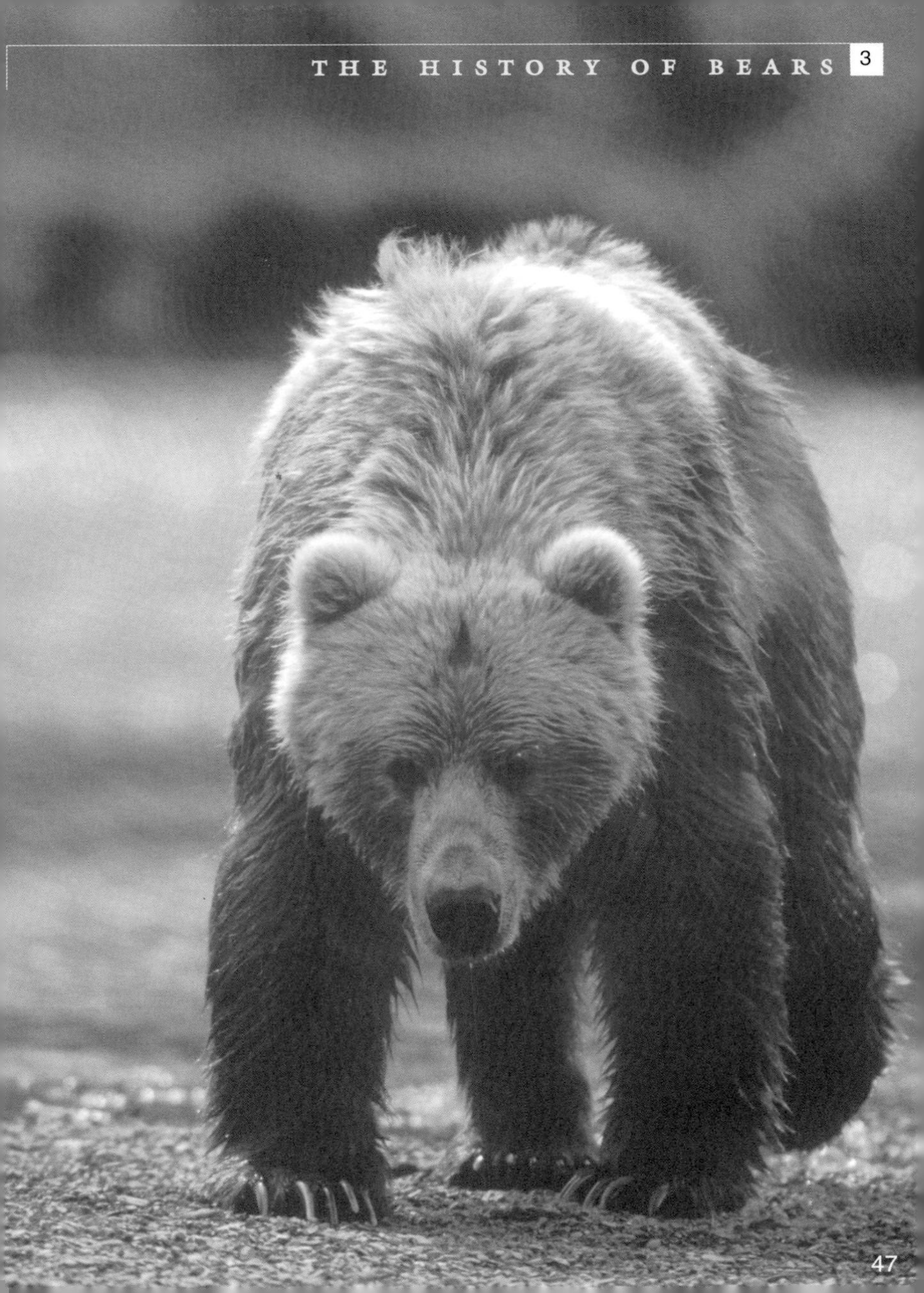

hunting was becoming popular with a wider variety of hunters, but subsistence harvests dwindled as most local residents lost their taste for bear meat. In spite of the more restrictive hunting regulations, biologists continued to be concerned with overharvests, and they noted that, between 1965 and 1976, there had been a significant decline in the average skull size of bears killed by hunters on Kodiak (94). Conflicts between bears and hunters of ungulates on the archipelago were also increasing as deer and elk populations increased and as harvest of these animals became more popular with hunters.

Aside from being seen as predators or as hunted prey, Kodiak bears were being viewed in a different manner by more and more people. One of the first popular published accounts to explore bear and human interactions from the Kodiak bear's perspective gained nationwide exposure when *Monarch of Deadman Bay* was published in 1969 (95).

Bear viewing and photography had been popular in places such as Yellowstone National Park since the turn of the century; in Alaska, territorial and state regulations between 1932 and 1967 mandated that all nonresident bear photographers be accompanied by registered big game guides. Several areas in Alaska attracted bears and photographers. In 1973, McNeil River State Game Sanctuary became the first area to establish a formal viewing program with limited entry for visitors (96). Members of the public and Kodiak National Wildlife Refuge staff expressed concern that, in spite of the worldwide recognition of Kodiak's bears, there was no portion of the refuge where bears were truly protected. Alaska Department of Fish and Game files show that, in 1976, refuge staff began exploring ways to close the Karluk River drainage to all bear hunting, either through the Board of Game process or through federal action.

To address the changing relationships with and uses of bears, the Alaska Department of Fish and Game developed a series of draft management plans for bears on the Kodiak Archipelago (97). The northern islands were divided into three separate management areas; Kodiak was also divided into three areas. Each of the areas was proposed to be managed for healthy bear populations, and research and other scientific studies were specifically endorsed in most. The management goal for southwestern Kodiak Island and for northern Afognak, Shuyak, Ban, and Marmot islands was to provide an opportunity to hunt brown bears under aesthetically pleasing conditions. Objectives were developed to minimize conflicts among hunters, maintain pristine habitat, and design hunting seasons that would maintain a high proportion of males in the harvest. The management goal for northeastern Kodiak Island and for southern Afognak and Raspberry islands was to provide the greatest opportunity to participate in hunting brown bears. Objectives in these areas included enhancing hunter access; reducing bear conflicts with livestock and people, and increasing public awareness of bear behavior. In the northeastern portion of Kodiak Island, it was acknowledged that the bear population was to be maintained, but at a level below the carrying capacity of the habitat.

Two areas, Karluk Lake on Kodiak Island and Portage Lake on Afognak Island, were proposed to be managed primarily to provide opportunities to view, photograph, and nonconsumptively enjoy bears. Management objectives included regulating the number and activities of visitors to protect bears from disturbance, encouraging adequate salmon escapement to support a high population of bears, and encouraging public viewing and photography of bears. Plans for each of the viewing areas also included objectives that would have allowed hunter harvest at a time when it would not conflict with viewing or photographing opportunities. In spite of the effort and public input involved in developing these and other wildlife management plans throughout the state, the Alaska Board of Game failed to accept the proposals, and no comprehensive bear-management plan for Kodiak was promulgated.

Commercial logging began on Afognak Island in 1977. By the end of the century, more than 1,000 miles of roads connected timber-harvesting areas on the island.

WILDERNESS AND CLEARCUTS

There were few new bear research activities during the 1970s, but biologists continued to estimate population trends by flying annual bear surveys along salmon spawning streams and alpine feeding areas (98), and radio-collared bears near Karluk Lake were monitored to delineate movement and habitat use patterns (99).

In 1972, the U.S. Fish and Wildlife Service completed a review of lands to potentially be designated as Wilderness Areas on Kodiak, recommending that as much as 97 percent of the refuge qualified as Wilderness under the guidelines of the Wilderness Act (100). None of those areas received formal designation because of concerns about the impending Native selections under ANCSA, but the Service opted to protect the integrity of the habitat in the refuge by managing most of it as if it had been designated a Wilderness Area. In 1975, the Service administratively designated the 88,000-acre Mt. Glottof Research Natural Area, an area stretching from Mt. Glottof to the alpine plateaus above Uganik Lake. It encompassed the alpine feeding habitat for brown bears and was also expected to provide an area for future research on bear summer feeding habits and habitats (101).

Afognak Island, which had been set aside as a Afognak Island Forest and Fish Culture Reserve in 1892 and managed as a bear sanctuary from 1932 through 1940, was subject to a drastically different management direction in the 1970s. The USDA Forest Service started planning the Perenosa Timber Sale in 1966 to "further establish Afognak Island as an integral part of the timber-management plan for Chugach National Forest." The plan also considered state timberlands on Shuyak and Kodiak islands as "potential economic opportunity for the development of a new timber-based industry in Alaska" (102). In 1968, timber in the proposed timber sale area was sold at public auction. The successful bidder planned to ship the unprocessed logs to Kodiak and build a mill at Frye Island in Woman's Bay.

Many local citizens were surprised by the plan to renew logging on Afognak after the 25-year hiatus since the military logging operation during World War II. They were also opposed to the plan to employ clearcut harvesting, noting the slow regeneration times for trees that had been previously cut from the island, and they voiced their opinions in the local newspaper. In response to these protests, and because of the newly established National Environmental Policy Act, the Forest Service delayed the sale and drafted an Environmental Impact Statement (103). The plan proposed setting aside, as locales that would not be logged, the Red Peaks Scenic Area on northwestern Afognak Island and an adjacent area to the south called the Paramanof Research Natural

Area. Forest Service staff worked with other agencies to conduct field reconnaissance efforts and to develop ways to efficiently harvest the timber while minimizing impacts on water resources, salmon, bears, and other wildlife. Projected impacts on bears included disturbance by logging activities and road traffic, disruption of salmon feeding areas, increased hunter access, and increased bear-human encounters resulting in bears being killed in defense of life or property. Finally, in 1975, the Forest Service began construction of a logging road between Kazakof (Danger) Bay and Discoverer Bay, and timber harvesting began in 1977.

Under ANCSA's provisions, the Native villages of Afognak, Kodiak, and Ouzinkie selected many of the prime forest lands on Afognak Island, as well as many of the coastal areas. In 1978, Koncor Forest Products began managing timber harvests on Kodiak and Ouzinkie lands. In 1979, Afognak Native Corporation took over management of its recently acquired lands.

Passage of the Alaska National Interest Lands Conservation Act (ANILCA) (Public Law 96-487) on December 2, 1980, added the northwestern portion of Afognak Island to the Kodiak National Wildlife Refuge, but it also curtailed the Forest Service's management on the island. In subsequent years, the rate of timber harvest was greatly accelerated over original projections made under Forest Service management. The new managers were not restricted by the same environmental constraints as were the federal managers, and they had more options to harvest timber in an economically efficient manner. State and federal agency staff were less influential in modifying harvest practices to minimize impacts on bears and other wildlife. Agency staff and corporation representatives readily debated the impacts of logging on bears in various areas; unfortunately, however, neither had objective data on population densities, movement patterns, reproduction, or mortality before, during, or after logging operations.

DAM IT

While the Forest Service was considering the Perenosa Timber Sale, the Federal Energy Regulatory Commission authorized study for a potential hydroelectric project at Terror Lake and Kizhuyak Bay on north Kodiak Island. The Kodiak Electric Association first proposed the Terror Lake hydro project in 1965 to supplement the increasing demand for power in Kodiak; soon after environmental

The Terror Lake hydroelectric project was the first major alteration of inland habitat on Kodiak Island. To mitigate the impacts of the project on bears, a five-year research project was conducted, and a $500,000 trust fund was established. Overall, there were few negative impacts from the hydroelectric project on the bears, and the trust was used to fund habitat acquisition and continued research.

studies were initiated, however, activities at the local U.S. Navy base diminished, and the need for additional power was reduced. The base was closed in May 1972, and the hydro project was held in abeyance. In the mid-1970s, the price of petroleum soared in response to a perceived worldwide shortage of oil reserves. The increasing costs of diesel-electric generation, along with revitalization of base activities by the U.S. Coast Guard and a booming fishing economy in Kodiak demanding more electricity, resurrected serious consideration of the project in 1977 (104).

In 1979, the Federal Energy Regulatory Commission began working on an environmental impact statement for the proposed Terror Lake hydro project. The project was to include an earthen dam on Terror Lake in the Kodiak National Wildlife Refuge and a six-mile-long tunnel through a mountain ridge to a penstock and powerhouse in the Kizhuyak River drainage. A 16-mile-long powerline was to connect the powerhouse with the city of Kodiak (104a). Preliminary studies suggested that the project would have several negative impacts on bears near the project, including disrupting denning and feeding areas, altering movement patterns, increasing strife and competition among bears, and escalating bear-human encounters (105).

The proposed project was to be the first significant invasion of inland bear habitat on Kodiak, and agencies and developers were faced with a lack of objective bear data, as had been the case with Afognak logging operations. To address the opposition encountered from the public and agencies, a mitigation settlement was negotiated in 1981 among three national conservation organizations and government agencies. The settlement was precedent setting in its scope, providing for studies of project impacts on salmon, mountain goats *(Oreamnos americanus)*, and bears during the three years of construction and two years of operation of the project. It also set aside most of the state and Kodiak Island Borough lands on the Shearwater Peninsula to be managed as wildlife habitat (and included a livestock-grazing prohibition) and established the Kodiak

Brown Bear Research and Habitat Maintenance Trust (referred to as the Kodiak Brown Bear Trust).

The trust was started with an initial investment by the Alaska Power Authority of $500,000, to be administered by four appointed trustees, including a representative from the national conservation organizations that were instrumental in the mitigation settlement (106). Developers of the hydro project also agreed to adopt food-storage and garbage disposal practices that would minimize bear encounters, to train all construction and operation personnel in bear-safety procedures, to fund an on-site environmental monitor from the U.S. Fish and Wildlife Service, to eliminate plans for an access road from the city of Kodiak, and to remove proposals to erect recreational cabins near project features. Construction of the Terror Lake hydro project commenced in the spring of 1982, coincident with initiation of a bear research project by Alaska Department of Fish and Game staff.

In the end, the forethought and planning were successful, and there were few negative impacts on bears that could be directly related to the Terror Lake hydro project. During that bear-research project, researchers maintained radio transmitters on an average of 36 bears per year, which yielded 4,792 bear relocations. Information gleaned from these tracked bears, and from unmarked bears that were seen by researchers and construction personnel, indicated that bears resided near the project and used approximately the same areas each year, making only minor shifts to areas with dense cover during construction. There was a reduction in bear use of alpine areas near the project during construction, but bears seemed to return soon afterward. Impacts on denning were less than predicted because most bears denned in areas away from project features (107). No bears were killed by hydro project personnel during construction, and threatening bear encounters were rare. A contractor was cited after bears were attracted to a camp by improper food and garbage storage during construction, but the situation was soon rectified after an out-of-court settlement was reached (108).

INCREASING KNOWLEDGE

Human alteration of bear habitat on Kodiak and Afognak islands spurred renewed interest and funding for bear research on the archipelago. In 1983, the U.S. Fish and Wildlife Service stationed a bear researcher at the Kodiak refuge, the first such dedicated research position since the inception of the refuge. A close bond was forged between the Service and Alaska Department of Fish and Game staffs, resulting in a surge of baseline and applied bear research on Kodiak through the 1980s and 1990s. Extensive use of radiotelemetry on bears living near Terror Lake (109), on southwestern Kodiak Island (110a-c), on the Aliulik Peninsula (111), and on the Spiridon Peninsula revealed denning, feeding, movement, and reproductive history patterns. Lip tattoos and ear tags were applied to 401 bears between 1982 and 1997 to investigate mortality rates and movements of bears that were not radio-collared (112a-b).

Another significant event for bears in the early 1980s was a surge in the deer populations throughout the archipelago. By that time, deer had occupied all available habitat with a population estimated to be in excess of 100,000 (113). Deer hunting also increased, reaching a peak harvest in 1987 with an estimated 13,791 deer killed by 6,022 hunters. Some bears actively preyed on deer, especially when they were concentrated on winter and late spring ranges along the coast, but in most cases such predation seemed opportunistic at best. Bears' use of deer carcasses and offal, however, was a different story.

Deer hunting seasons on the Kodiak archipelago were liberal, with bag limits of as many as seven deer in most areas; approximately 90 percent of the deer harvest occurred in October, November, and December. During that same autumn period, food resources for bears diminish as vegetation gets coarse, berries deteriorate, and fish runs dwindle. Prior to entering dens, Kodiak bears may aggressively seek any food they can find in an effort to make final preparations for their winter fast. The combination of thousands of hunters quietly stalking, packing meat, and camping within the habitat of dense populations of bears looking for food was a lethal recipe. Bear-human encounters increased steadily, and rumors spread that bears were learning that gunshots were like "dinner bells" (114).

Although such behaviors were never substantiated, it was evident that individual bears quickly discovered techniques to claim hunter-killed deer both in the field and at campsites. Increasing encounters translated into more bears being killed in defense of life or property (115). An investigation near Zachar Bay used radio-collared bears and hunter questionnaires to estimate the extent of the bear-human conflicts. The results of this study indicated that as many as 21 percent of the hunters had a threatening encounter with a bear while deer hunting, and as many as 26 percent lost deer meat to bears (116). Although there were suggestions to reduce deer seasons and bag limits, and to reduce sport harvests of bears in specific areas, managers opted to forego changes in regulations. Hunter education efforts were increased, with an emphasis on ways to avoid bear encounters and nonlethal methods to handle them should they occur.

Perhaps the most significant result of the plethora of research in the 1980s and 1990s was development of an objective method of measuring bear population densities and trends on specific parts of Kodiak Island. In cooperation with bear researchers throughout Alaska, biologists on Kodiak refined a traditional method known as "capture-mark-recapture" using radiotelemetry and aerial surveys (117). Application of this technique to several parts of Kodiak, along with some extrapolation to the rest of the archipelago, provided the first refined estimate of bear numbers (2,980) and density (0.62 bears per square mile) (118a-b). Unfortunately the technique was prohibitively expensive for routine monitoring of population trends. With continued research, the methodology was modified to reduce the costs dramatically without sacrificing accuracy (119), and Kodiak wildlife managers finally had a way to monitor the status of the bear population.

Increasing human uses of the archipelago and increased knowledge about Kodiak bears prompted more and more restrictive hunting regulations. In 1978, the winter hunting season along the Kodiak road system was eliminated; in 1979, hunters were no longer allowed to hunt during the same day they had been flying. Fall hunting seasons were reduced in 1978, 1979, and 1984 in an effort to reduce the number of adult females killed. Starting in 1978, hunters were restricted to a 15-day hunt period. Bear-hunting seasons on Afognak were reduced in 1977, 1979, 1983, and 1984. In 1987, Afognak and the other northern islands, along with a portion of Kodiak Island between Kizhuyak River and Saltery Cove, were removed from the registration permit area, and permits were limited and issued by lottery (drawing permits).

OIL SPILLS, SETTLEMENT MONEY, AND HABITAT ACQUISITION

Kodiak beaches were subjected to periodic contamination by petroleum products beginning in the late 1800s, when oil became a more popular fuel for powering boats and heating homes. During

World War II, the frequency and size of oil, gasoline, and paving material discharges into Kodiak waters, either accidently or intentionally, increased significantly as the volume of these petroleum products in the area grew and people's concern about environmental damage waned. In February 1970, a major oil spill hit the beaches of northeastern Kodiak, killing large numbers of birds and seals and soiling sea lions. The cause of the spill was suspected to be ships discharging oily ballast water near the island. As politicians called for "immediate and effective state action" and "a full federal investigation," it was evident that public tolerance of these practices had changed (120). These spills probably had little or no impact on the bear populations, but they were precursors to another oil-related event that accelerated the continuing evolution of the relationship between bears and people on Kodiak.

On March 24, 1989, the infamous *Exxon Valdez* impaled itself at high tide on Bligh Reef in Prince William Sound. As the tide receded, the crippled tanker disgorged 11 million gallons of its crude oil cargo into the pristine waters of the sound. Winds and currents spread the oil throughout the sound within the first week, and soon thereafter it continued its deadly dispersion to the south and west, eventually engulfing portions of the Kenai Peninsula, the Alaska Peninsula, and the Kodiak islands (121). The oil washed through large sea bird rookeries just as the spring migration was commencing and persisted through the summer

Biologists were concerned that bears foraging in the oiled intertidal areas would be adversely affected as they scavenged bird and mammal carcasses that washed up on beaches or that their coats would be coated by oil, possibly resulting in hypothermia or poisoning.

season. Marine mammals, including sea otters, seals, sea lions, and whales, were soiled and poisoned. Coastal birds and mammals were also affected because feeding and resting areas were tainted. Biologists were concerned that bears foraging in the oiled intertidal areas would be adversely affected as they scavenged bird and mammal carcasses that washed up on beaches or that their coats would be coated by oil, possibly resulting in hypothermia or poisoning.

The magnitude of the spill, coupled with the inherent natural beauty of the affected area, caught the attention of the world. Reporters, corporate and agency representatives, politicians, and spill clean-up crews deluged the area. Kodiak's coastal waters were devoid of the usual level of commercial fishing because the Alaska Department of Fish and Game closed most salmon seasons in the area, but the intensity of human activity on beaches and near shore waters was raised to a fever pitch by clean-up crews. Thousands of people, many of whom had no experiences with brown bears, were living and working in some of the best bear habitat in the state. Resource managers recognized that the impact of those workers on the bears was potentially greater than the impact of the oil itself. Exxon Co. and its contractors recognized there was potential liability if its employees were injured by bears, so they worked closely with Alaska Department of Fish and Game biologists to develop mandatory bear-safety training for everyone involved with the clean-up efforts (122).

The estimated death toll from the oil spill included 250,000 sea birds, 2,800 sea otters, 300 harbor seals (*Phoca vitulina*), 250 bald eagles (*Haliaeetus leucocephalus*), and 22 killer whales (*Orcinus orca*) (123). The closure of commercial salmon fishing in many areas allowed an overabundance of sockeye to return to some lakes. Although this was a boon for bears in 1989, there was some habitat disruption, which resulted in a decline in juvenile growth of sockeye and reduced runs in some subsequent years (124).

Bears did not appear to be directly harmed by the spill, although some were displaced from traditional feeding and traveling areas by clean-up crews (125). No one was injured by a bear, and only two bears (neither from Kodiak) were killed by people associated with the clean-up. To mitigate the adverse impacts of the spill, Exxon Co. reached a settlement agreement with the state and federal governments for $1 billion. A six-member trustee council was established to disburse the funds ". . . for the purposes of restoring, replacing, enhancing, or acquiring the equivalent of natural resources injured as a result of the oil spill . . ." (126).

Paradoxically, the impacts of the oil spill and the subsequent clean-up and settlement proved to be beneficial to bears on Kodiak. Bear-safety training exposed thousands of workers to information on bear life history, behavior, and habitat requirements, and the international media raised the consciousness of people around the world to the fragility of the coastal ecosystem of southcentral Alaska. Media attention also highlighted the controversy of "bear habitat versus Native lands" that had been festering on the Kodiak islands. Fears raised in the 1970s, after the passage of ANCSA, were being realized. Natives now owned lands surrounding riparian areas that produced more than 70 percent of the salmon in the archipelago (127), and many of these landowners were anxious to profit from their inholdings. Provisions within ANCSA, which restricted uses of these lands, were being challenged, and threats to brown bears and their habitat were serious.

Political pressure mounted to preserve Kodiak's pristine habitats, and money from the Exxon Valdez settlement fund was the obvious source for funding land acquisitions. Many landowners were supportive of preserving lands in their natural state so that they could continue to enjoy the abundant resources passed down from their ancestors while also being paid fair market value for their lands. Kodiak National Wildlife Refuge was also enthusiastic to renew its management authority over lands that had previously been part of the refuge, and the state and the public were pleased with renewed public access to the lands. By the close of the 1990s, about 80 percent of the Kodiak National Wildlife Refuge lands that had been lost because of ANCSA were reinstated in to the refuge, either through direct purchase or by means of conservation ease-ments (128). Lands were also purchased on Afognak and Shuyak islands and transferred into state ownership.

Settlement funds were used for most of the large parcel acquisitions, but small parcels and numerous private inholdings were bought by a coalition of groups coordinated by the Kodiak Brown Bear Trust. The trust had been created as part of the Terror Lake hydro settlement, and money from it had been used to fund several bear research projects on Kodiak. To facilitate habitat acquisition, trustees and staff worked with landowners and agencies to broker mutually acceptable agreements. They also educated a wide variety of private organizations and individuals about the plight of the bears' habitat and the opportunity to conserve it. Response was positive, and contributions were provided by people with diverse interests—from hunters to wildlife viewers. Once again, the mystique and reputation of Kodiak's bears served to protect them and their homes from detrimental impacts by people.

HARVEST STABILITY AND INCREASING NONCONSUMPTIVE USE

From the late 1980s through the 1990s, the human population of the archipelago remained nearly constant at about 14,500. Bear harvests also stayed relatively stable, with about 160 bears (approximately 70 percent males) killed by sport hunters each year (129). Hunting regulations changed little, with minor adjustments being made to accommodate legal challenges to the state's exclusive guide areas. There were also regulation changes to adhere to provisions of ANILCA that mandated that subsistence hunters have a priority use of wildlife resources on federal lands. In 1985, the state initiated a subsistence hunt on Kodiak from April 1

Bear viewing has always been popular on Kodiak, but public demand for bear viewing areas increased in the 1980s. Research on Kodiak indicated that structured bear viewing programs have little adverse impact on bears, whereas unrestricted bear viewing near critical feeding areas may be detrimental to them

through 15. This hunt was in place until 1987, and no bears were harvested. The state's attempt to implement subsistence priorities was met with legal challenges from Alaska residents as well as from the federal government. On July 1, 1990, the federal government assumed responsibility for management of subsistence taking of fish and wildlife on federal public lands in Alaska, thus ushering in an era of dual management (130). In 1996, a federal subsistence hunt began for Kodiak Island villagers. The seasons extended December 1–15 and April 1–May 15. The number of permits available was limited, and successful hunters were required to salvage all edible meat from the bears they harvested.

Kodiak bear populations also appeared to be stable in most areas during the 1980s and 1990s. New management guidelines established in 1987 tasked managers to

• maintain a stable brown bear population that will sustain an annual harvest of 150 bears composed of at least 60 percent males,

• maintain diversity in the sex and age composition of the brown bear population, with adult bears of all ages represented in the population and in the harvest, and

• limit human-caused mortality of female brown bears to a level consistent with maintaining maximum productivity.

Periodic intensive aerial surveys were included in the refuge's management budget, and the annual flights were scheduled to be joint efforts with Alaska Department of Fish and Game biologists. When biologists noted indications of a potential overharvest of adult female bears on southwestern Kodiak, they worked closely with guides to reduce this harvest by implementing a regulation in 1995 that restricted guided hunters to male bears or females with a skull size of at least 15 inches long or 9 inches wide. Failure to meet these minimums in these areas resulted in the loss of a permit for the next hunting season. The regulation proved effective, and no overall reductions in permits were necessary, although some guides did lose permits in some years because of taking restricted bears (131).

In 1987, the Kodiak National Wildlife Refuge completed its first Comprehensive Conservation Plan (132). That plan and the supplemental Public Use Management Plan (133) addressed conservation and management issues on refuge lands. One of the obvious changes occurring during the development of these plans was the rapid expansion of bear viewing and photography on the archipelago. Although these activities had always been popular, the publicity the islands and the bears received during and after the oil spill motivated people to come and see the bears in their natural habitat. To address this public demand, a trial bear-viewing program, modeled after the McNeil River Sanctuary program, was administered by the refuge at Dog Salmon River in 1990 and 1991 and at O'Malley River in 1992 and 1994 (134). The O'Malley program was cancelled after 1994 because of a legal challenge to the procedures used in awarding the bear-viewing concession, and the area was closed to all human access during the summer months. A guided bear-viewing program was operated by a private operator on Koniag Corporation land at Thumb River on Karluk Lake from 1995 through 1999.

Refuge staff investigated bear and human interactions at the O'Malley and the Thumb viewing areas during a variety of management scenarios and concluded that bears could tolerate bear-viewing programs along these fishing streams as long as the human activities were predictable and restricted to specific areas (135). Unrestricted "nonconsumptive" use, however, could be detrimental to bears because of direct encounters with people or because of displacement to less suitable habitat. To address these concerns, refuge staff restricted areas and techniques that could be used by commercial bear-viewing operators on the refuge during critical times.

ON TO THE FUTURE

As the millennium waned, Kodiak bears and their human neighbors faced yet another challenge. During the summer of 1999, as many problem bears (eight) were killed near the city of Kodiak as had been killed in the previous nine years combined. Kodiak Island villages also had more bear problems than ever, and deer hunters reported a dramatic increase in bear encounters island-wide, including the first fatal mauling in more than 70 years. The rash of bear confrontations was caused by a disastrous failure of berries, on which the bears depended for food in early August. The worst weather in 40 years struck the island during the winter of 1998-99 and damaged the berry bushes so severely that they could not produce fruit. In their search for food, some bears found garbage, livestock, and dog food, bringing them in closer than usual contact with people.

The reaction to these bear encounters by residents, visitors, and government agents reflected the increased tolerance and knowledge of the populace. Kodiak residents requested and received bear education programs for school children, for public television and radio, and for ethnic groups. Waste management was enhanced by installation of bear-resistant dumpsters in rural areas on the Kodiak road system and by increased enforcement of litter laws. A previously installed electric fence around the community landfill was reinforced, vegetative cover within the fence was removed, and garbage was buried more frequently. Deer and

When faced with increasing bear-human conflicts during the summer of 1999, Kodiak residents responded by seeking ways to live with the bears instead of indiscriminately annihilating them.

elk hunters were alerted to the potentially dangerous situation. When the fatal mauling occurred,
media were quick to point out the hunter's errors
rather than blame the bear; law enforcement and
wildlife officials did not hunt or kill the bear responsible for the
mauling. All in all, the community pulled together
to address the problems and everyone, including
the bears, benefited (136)

Most of the people of Kodiak were proud of
the fact that they lived with the largest bears, and
one of the densest populations of bears, in the
world. They were willing to take an active role in
ensuring continued coexistence. This increased
"ownership" of the bears also resulted in a call to
have a citizens advisory committee work closely
with the Alaska Department of Fish and Game,
with the cooperation of the Kodiak National Wildlife
Refuge, to develop a management plan address-
ing the wide variety of issues that impact bears,
including hunting, habitat, and viewing.

The resulting Kodiak Archipelago Bear
Conservation and Management Plan (137) was
crafted over a several month period by a group of
representatives from 12 diverse user groups. The
Alaska Department of Fish and Game funded the
project and provided technical and logistical
support, but they did not attempt to influence the
group's decisions. After hearing from a variety of
experts from agencies and extensive public input,
the group developed over 270 recommendations
for Kodiak bear management and conservation.
Most impressively, in spite of the diversity of view-

The future looks
bright for the
continuing
existence of
the bears of the
Kodiak Islands.

points expressed by members of the group, all of the recommendations were by consensus.

The underlying themes of the recommendations were continued conservation of the bear population at its current level, increased education programs to teach people how to live with bears on Kodiak, and protection of bear habitat with allowances for continued human use of the archipelago. Although the group was advisory in nature, government management agencies expressed a commitment to work to implement all of the regulations that were feasible and within their legal jurisdictions. How this maturing relationship between bears and people will evolve remains to be seen, but the future looks bright for the continuing existence of the bears of the Kodiak Islands.

LITERATURE CITED

1. Buck, E. H., W. J. Wilson, L. S. Lau, C. Liburd, and H. W. Searby. 1975. *Kadyak—A Background for Living. Arctic Information and Data Center*, University of Alaska, Anchorage, Anchorage, Alaska.

2. Kurten, B. 1976. *The Cave Bear Story: Life and Death of a Vanished Animal.* Columbia University Press, New York, New York

3. Waits, L., D. Paetkau, C. Strobeck, and R. H. Ward. 1998. "A comparison of genetic diversity in North American brown bears." *Ursus* 10:307–314.

4. Merriam, C.H. 1918. Review of the grizzly and big brown bears of North American. U.S. Department of Agriculture, Bureau of Biological Survey, Washington, D.C. North American Fauna Number 41. (pp. 126–127).

5. Rausch, R. L. 1969. "Origin of the terrestrial mammalian fauna of the Kodiak Archipelago. in Karlstrom," T. N. V., and G. R. Ball, editors. *The Kodiak Island Refugium: Its geology, flora, fauna, and history.* Ryerson Press, Toronto, Canada. (The Boreal Institute, University of Alberta).

6. Steffian, A. Alutiiq Museum, personal communication, 2000.

7. Rausch, R. L. 1969. "Origin of the terrestrial mammalian fauna of the Kodiak Archipelago. in Karlstrom," T. N. V., and G. R. Ball, editors. *The Kodiak Island Refugium: Its geology, flora, fauna, and history.* Ryerson Press, Toronto, Canada. (The Boreal Institute, University of Alberta).

8. Petroff, 1884 in Hrdlicka, A. 1944. *The Anthropology of Kodiak Island.* The Winstar Institute of Anatomy and Biology, Philadelphia, Pennsylvania.

9. Clark, D. W. 1968. Koniag Prehistory [Ph.D. Thesis]. University of Wisconsin.

10a. Hrdlicka, A. 1944. *The Anthropology of Kodiak Island.* The Winstar Institute of Anatomy and Biology, Philadelphia, Pennsylvania.

10b. P. Saltonstall, Alutiiq Museum, personal communication, 2000

11. Van Daele L. J., J. R. Morgart, M. T. Hinkes, S. D. Kovach, J. W. Denton, and R. H. Kaycon. 2001. 'Grizzlies, Eskimos, and Biologists: Cross-cultural bear management in southwest Alaska." *Ursus* 12:141-152.

12. Clark, D. W. 1968. Koniag Prehistory [Ph.D. Thesis]. University of Wisconsin.

13. Jordan, D. S. 1898. *Seal and Salmon Fisheries and General Resources of Alaska. Volume IV.* U.S. Government Printing Office, Washington, D.C.

14. Tikhmenev, P. A. 1978. *A History of the Russian-American Company.* Pierce, R. A., and A. S. Donnelly, editors. University of Washington Press, Seattle, Washington.

15. Jordan, D. S. 1898. *Seal and Salmon Fisheries and General Resources of Alaska. Volume IV.* U.S. Government Printing Office, Washington, D.C.

16. Huggins, E. L. 1981. *Kodiak and Afognak Life,* 1868–1870. The Limestone Press, Kingston, Ontario, Canada.

17. Jordan, D. S. 1898. *Seal and Salmon Fisheries and General Resources of Alaska. Volume IV.* U.S. Government Printing Office, Washington, D.C.

18. Alaska Fisheries and Fur Industries. 1913. Baranov Museum archives, Kodiak, Alaska.

19. Roppel, P. 1986. *Salmon from Kodiak.* Alaska Historical Commission, Anchorage, Alaska.

20. Roppel, P. 1986. *Salmon from Kodiak.* Alaska Historical Commission, Anchorage, Alaska.

21. Roppel, P. 1986. *Salmon from Kodiak.* Alaska Historical Commission, Anchorage, Alaska.

22. Roppel, P. 1986. *Salmon from Kodiak.* Alaska Historical Commission, Anchorage, Alaska.

23. Robards, F. C., and J. G. King. 1966. Nesting and productivity of bald eagles in Southeast Alaska—1966. U.S. Department of the Interior, Bureau of Sport Fisheries and Wildlife, Juneau, Alaska.

24. Ballenger, B., Alaska Dept. of Fish & Game, personal communication, 2000.

25. Chaffin, T. 1967. *Koniag to King Crab.* Desert News Press.

26. Chaffin, Y., T. Hampton-Krieger, and M. Rostad. 1983. *Alaska's Konyag Country.* Pratt Publishing.

27. Chaffin, Y., T. Hampton-Krieger, and M. Rostad. 1983. *Alaska's Konyag Country.* Pratt Publishing.

28. Baier, L. E. 1993. The Boone and Crockett Club: A 106-year prospective. 3-28 in Records of Big Game of North American. The Boone and Crockett Club, Missoula, Montana

29. Merriam, C. H. 1896. *Ursus middendorffi.* 69–71. Proceedings of the Biological Society of Washington.

30. Grinnel, G.B. 1995. *Alaska 1899: Essays from the Harriman Expedition.* University of Washington Press, Seattle, Washington

31. Grinnell, G. B. 1904. *American Big Game In Its Haunts.* Forest and Stream Publishing, New York, New York.

32. Whitney, E. 1912. *The King Bear of Kadiak Island.* The Boys Big Game Series. Reilly & Lee, Chicago, Illinois.

33. Buck, E. H., W. J. Wilson, L. S. Lau, C. Liburd, and H. W. Searby. 1975. Kadyak—A Background for Living. Arctic Information and Data Center; University of Alaska, Anchorage, Anchorage, Alaska.

34. Chaffin, Y., T. Hampton-Krieger, and M. Rostad. 1983. *Alaska's Konyag Country.* Pratt Publishing.

35. Martin, G. C. 1913. "The recent eruption of Katmai Volcano in Alaska." *National Geographic.* XXIV (2): pp. 131–181.

36. Martin, G. C. 1913. "The recent eruption of Katmai Volcano in Alaska." *National Geographic.* XXIV (2): pp. 131–181.

37. Martin, G. C. 1913. "The recent eruption of Katmai Volcano in Alaska." *National Geographic.* XXIV (2): pp. 131–181.

38. Roppel, P. 1982. *Alaska's salmon hatcheries*, 1891–1959. National Marine Fisheries Service, Portland, Oregon.

39. Roppel, P. 1986. *Salmon from Kodiak.* Alaska Historical Commission, Anchorage, Alaska

40. Palmer, L. J. 1938. Wildlife problems on Kodiak Island. Alaska Department of Fish and Game, Kodiak, Alaska.

41. Burris, O. E., and D. E. McKnight. 1973. Game transplants in Alaska. Alaska Department of Fish and Game, Juneau, Alaska. (Technical Bulletin No. 4).

42. Batchelor, R. F. 1965. The Roosevelt Elk in Alaska: its ecology and management. Alaska Department of Fish and Game; Federal Aid in Wildlife Restoration, Vol. V. Project W-6-R-5. Work Plan D, Juneau, Alaska.

43. Burris, O. E., and D. E. McKnight. 1973. Game transplants in Alaska. Alaska Department of Fish and Game, Juneau, Alaska. (Technical Bulletin No. 4).

44. Alaska Game Commission. 1929. Laws and regulations relating to game, land, and fur-bearing animals and birds in Alaska. U.S. Department of Agriculture, Bureau of Biological Survey, Juneau, Alaska.

45. Alaska Game Commision. 1932. Laws and regulations relating to game, land, and fur-bearing animals and birds in Alaska. U.S. Department of Agriculture, Bureau of Biological Survey, Juneau, Alaska.

46. Palmer, L. J. 1938. Wildlife problems on Kodiak Island. Alaska Department of Fish and Game, Kodiak, Alaska.

47. Palmer, L. J. 1938. Wildlife problems on Kodiak Island. Alaska Department of Fish and Game, Kodiak, Alaska.

48. Palmer, L. J. 1938. Wildlife problems on Kodiak Island. Alaska Department of Fish and Game, Kodiak, Alaska.

49. Sarber, H. R. 1939. Report of the Kodiak brown bear control project. Alaska State Game Commission, Alaska Department of Fish and Game files, Kodiak, Alaska.

50. Sarber, H. R. 1939. Report of the Kodiak brown bear control project. Alaska State Game Commission, Alaska Department of Fish and Game files, Kodiak, Alaska.

51. Environmental Law Institute. 1977. *The Evolution of National Wildlife Law.* Council of Environmental Quality. U.S. Government Printing Office, Washington, D.C.

52. KNWR. 1971. Kodiak National Wildlife Refuge Annual Narrative Report–1971.U.S. Fish and Wildlife Service, Kodiak, Alaska.

53. Chaffin, Y., T. Hampton-Krieger, and M. Rostad. 1983. *Alaska's Konyag Country.* Pratt Publishing

54. Shuman, R. F. 1945. Monthly Report of Activities for the Section of Alaska Fisheries Investigations for July 1945. Alaska Department of Fish and Game, Kodiak, Alaska.

55. Shuman, R.F. 1947. Bear depredations on sockeye spawning populations in the Karluk River system, 1947. Alaska Department of Fish and Game, Kodiak, Alaska.

56. Clark, W. K. 1955. Bear Study—Karluk Lake. Kodiak National Wildlife Refuge, Kodiak, Alaska.

57. Hoffman, R. R., and J. E. Lutz. 1953. A plan for the management of the Kodiak brown bear. Report to the Kodiak National Wildlife Refuge, Kodiak, Alaska.

58. Hoffman, R. R., and J. E. Lutz. 1953. A plan for the management of the Kodiak brown bear. Report to the Kodiak National Wildlife Refuge, Kodiak, Alaska.

59. Clark, W. K. 1955. Bear Study—Karluk Lake. Kodiak National Wildlife Refuge, Kodiak, Alaska

60. Clark, W. K. 1955. Bear Study—Karluk Lake. Kodiak National Wildlife Refuge, Kodiak, Alaska

61. Clark, W.K., 1957a. Seasonal Food Habits of the Kodiak Bear. 145–149. Proceedings Wildlife Management Institute, Washington, D.C.

62. Shuman, R.F. 1947. Bear depredations on sockeye spawning populations in the Karluk River system, 1947. Alaska Department of Fish and Game, Kodiak, Alaska.

63. Dufresne, F. 1951. "Is Alaska's Kodiak Doomed?" *Field and Stream*. pp.30–31, 78–79.

64. Ford, C. 1953. "Is Alaska's Kodiak Doomed?" *Field and Stream*. March 1953. pp. 40–42, 137–140.

65. Ford, C. 1955. "Biggest bear on earth." *The Saturday Evening Post*. November 12, 1955. pp. 38–39, 110–113.

66. Ford, C. 1955. "Biggest bear on earth." *The Saturday Evening Post*. November 12, 1955. pp. 38–39, 110–113.

67. Fleming, E. J. 1958. "Do brown bears attack?" *Outdoor Life*. 122 (5): pp.41–43, 92–97.

68. Hoffman, R. R., D. L. Spencer, and E. F. Chatelain. 1953. Report of a reconnaissance to investigate the grazing potentials of livestock on the one-mile strip along the periphery of Kodiak Island, Alaska. Alaska Department of Fish and Game, Kodiak, Alaska.

69. Clark, W.K. 1957b. Supplemental Report to the Kodiak Refuge narrative report, September to December 1957—Karluk Lake Bear Study. Kodiak National Wildlife Refuge, Kodiak, Alaska.

70a. Troyer, W. A. 1961. The brown bear harvest in relation to management on Kodiak Islands. pp. 460–468. Proceedings of Twenty-sixth North American Wildlife Conference; Wildlife Management Institute, Washington, D.C.

70b. Woodworth, J. 1958. *The Kodiak Bear*. The Stackpole Company, Harrisburg, Pennsylvania.

71. Gard, R. 1971. Brown bear predation on sockeye salmon at Karluk Lake, Alaska. *J. Wildlife Management* 35:193–204.

72. Troyer, W.A. 1962. Size, distribution, structure, and harvest of a Kodiak bear population [M.S. Thesis]. Montana State University, Missoula, Montana.

73. Troyer, W. A., R. J. Hensel, and K. E. Durley. 1962. Live-trapping and handling of brown bears. *J. Wildlife Management* 26(3):330–331.

74. Berns, V. D., and R. J. Hensel. 1972. Radio tracking brown bears on Kodiak Island. 19–25. Proceedings of International Conference on Bear Research and Management.

75. Troyer, W.A. and R.J. Hensel. 1969. The brown bear of Kodiak Island. U.S. Bureau of Sport Fisheries and Wildlife. (unpublished).

76a. Erickson, A. W., H. W. Mossman, R. J. Hensel, and W. A. Troyer. 1968. The breeding biology of the male brown bear (*Ursus arctos*). *Zoological* 53(3):85–105.

76b. Gilbert, J. R. 1970. Reproductive biology of female Kodiak brown bear [M.S. Thesis]. University of Minnesota.

76c. Hensel, R. J., W. A. Troyer, and A. W. Erickson. 1969. "Reproduction in the female brown bear." *J. Wildlife Management* 33(2):357–365.

77. Troyer, W. A., and R. J. Hensel. 1964. "Behavior of female brown bears under stress." *J. Mammalogy* 45(3):488–489.

78. Troyer, W. A., and R. J. Hensel. 1962. "Cannibalism in brown bear." *Animal Behavior* 10:3–4.

79. Troyer, W.A. and R.J. Hensel. 1969. The brown bear of Kodiak Island. U.S. Bureau of Sport Fisheries and Wildlife. (unpublished).

80. Lentfer, J. W., R. J. Hensel, L. H. Miller, L. P. Glenn, and V. D. Berns. 1972. Remarks on denning habitats of Alaska brown bears. Proceedings of the Second International Conference on Bear Research and Management, 1970; University of Calgary, Calgary, Alberta, Canada.

81. Eide, S. 1965. The nature of brown bear predation on cattle, Kodiak Island, Alaska. Anchorage, Alaska.

82. Eide, S. 1965. The nature of brown bear predation on cattle, Kodiak Island, Alaska. Anchorage, Alaska.

83. Eide, S. 1964. Kodiak bear-cattle relationships. Alaska Department of Fish and Game, Kodiak, Alaska.

84. Reardon, J. 1964. "The Kodiak Bear War." *Outdoor Life*. 134 (2): pp. 17–19, 70–76.

85. Reardon, J. 1964. "The Kodiak Bear War. *Outdoor Life*." 134 (2): pp. 17–19, 70–76.

86. J. Alexander to S.H. Eide, Alaska Department of Fish and Game, interagency memorandum, December 29, 1969.

87. J.A. Harper, letter to M.P. Cannon, Alaska Department of Fish and Game, 1970.

88. Fields, W. M. 2000. *Now it can be told.* Publication Consultants, Anchorage, Alaska.

89. Blackett, R. F. 1979. Establishment of Sockeye and Chinook salmon runs at Frazer Lake, Kodiak Island, Alaska. *J. Fisheries Research Board of Canada* 36(19):1265–1277.

90. Buck, E. H., W. J. Wilson, L. S. Lau, C. Liburd, and H. W. Searby. 1975. Kadyak—A Background for Living. Arctic Information and Data Center; University of Alaska, Anchorage, Anchorage, Alaska.

91. Hanley, P. T., J. E. Hemming, J. W. Morsell, T. A. Morehouse, L. E. Leask, and G. S. Harrison. 1981. Natural resource protection and petroleum development in Alaska. U.S. Fish and Wildlife Service, Office of Biological Services, Anchorage, Alaska. Report nr FWS/OBS-80-22

92. KNWR. 1971. Kodiak National Wildlife Refuge Annual Narrative Report–1971.U.S. Fish and Wildlife Service, Kodiak, Alaska.

93. Smith, R. B. 1981. Kodiak brown bear management, 1958–1980. Notes from an oral presentation to the Carnivore and Furbearer Conference; Fairbanks, Alaska: Alaska Department of Fish and Game.

94. KNWR. 1976. Kodiak National Wildlife Refuge Annual Narrative Report–1976. U.S. Fish and Wildlife Service, Kodiak, Alaska.

95. Caras, R. A. 1969. *Monarch of Deadman Bay—The Life and Death of a Kodiak Bear.* Little, Brown and Company, Boston, Massachusetts.

96. Walker, T., and L. Aumiller. 1993. *River of Bears.* Voyageur Press, Stillwater, Minnesota.

97. Alaska Department of Fish and Game. 1977. Alaska Wildlife Management Plans–Southwestern Alaska–Draft Proposal. Alaska Department of Fish and Game; Federal Aid in Wildlife Restoration, Project W-17-R, Juneau, Alaska.

98. Atwell, G., D. L. Boone, J. Gustafson, and V. D. Berns. 1980. Brown bear summer use of alpine habitat on Kodiak National Wildlife Refuge. 297-305. Proceedings of International Conference on Bear Research and Management.

99. Berns, V. D., G. C. Atwell, and D. L. Boone. 1980. Brown bear movements and habitat use at Karluk Lake, Kodiak Island. 293–296. Proceedings of International Conference on Bear Research and Management.

100. U.S. Fish and Wildlife Service. 1972. Kodiak National Wildlife Refuge Wilderness Review. U.S. Fish and Wildlife Service, Kodiak, Alaska.

101. KNWR. 1987. Kodiak National Wildlife Refuge Comprehensive Conservation Plan, Environmental Impact Statement, and Wilderness Review. U.S. Fish and Wildlife Service, Anchorage, Alaska.

102. USDA Forest Service. 1974. Perenosa Timber Sale—Revision and Reappraisal (Environmental Impact Statement, plus appendices). U.S. Department of Agriculture, Forest Service, Anchorage, Alaska.

103. USDA Forest Service. 1974. Perenosa Timber Sale—Revision and Reappraisal (Environmental Impact Statement, plus appendices). U.S. Department of Agriculture, Forest Service, Anchorage, Alaska.

104. Hickock, D. M., and W. J. Wilson. 1979. An assessment of environmental effects of construction and operation of the proposed Terror Lake hydroelectric facility, Kodiak, Alaska. University of Alaska, Anchorage, Arctic Environmental Information and Data Center, Anchorage, Alaska.

104a. Smith, R. B., and L. J. Van Daele. 1988. Terror Lake hydroelectric project, Kodiak Island, Alaska—Final report on brown bear studies (1982–1986). Alaska Department of Fish and Game, Kodiak, Alaska.

105. Spencer, D. L., and R. J. Hensel. 1980. As assessment of environmental effects on construction and operation of the proposed Terror Lake hydroelectric facility, Kodiak, Alaska. 100 pp. in Brown Bear Studies and Mountain Goat Studies. University of Alaska, Anchorage, Arctic Environmental Information and Data Center, Anchorage, Alaska.

106. Smith, R. B., and L. J. Van Daele. 1990. Impacts of hydroelectric development on brown bears, Kodiak Island, Alaska. pp. 93–103. Proceedings of International Conference on Bear Research and Management.

107. Van Daele, L. J.,V. G. Barnes, Jr., and R. B. Smith. 1990. Denning characteristics of brown bears on Kodiak Island, Alaska. pp. 257–267. Proceedings of International Conference on Bear Research and Management.

108. Smith, R. B., and L. J. Van Daele. 1990. Impacts of hydroelectric development on brown bears, Kodiak Island, Alaska. pp. 93–103. Proceedings of International Conference on Bear Research and Management.

109. Smith, R. B., and L. J. Van Daele. 1990. Impacts of hydroelectric development on brown bears, Kodiak Island, Alaska. pp. 93–103. Proceedings of International Conference on Bear Research and Management.

110a. Barnes, V. G., Jr. 1990. The influence of salmon availability on movements and range of brown bears on southwest Kodiak Island. 305-313. Proceedings of International Conference on Bear Research and Management.

110b. Barnes, V.G., Jr. and R.B. Smith. 1993. "Cub Adoption by Brown Bears, *Ursus arctos middendorffi,* on Kodiak Island, Alaska." *The Canadian Field-Naturalist* 107:365-367.

110c. Van Daele, L. J.,V. G. Barnes, Jr., and R. B. Smith. 1990. Denning characteristics of brown bears on Kodiak Island, Alaska. pp. 257–267. Proceedings of International Conference on Bear Research and Management.

111. Barnes, V. G., Jr., and R. B. Smith. 1997. Population ecology of brown bears on Aliulik Peninsula, Kodiak Island, Alaska. U.S. National Biological Service and Alaska Department of Game; Final Report to the National Fish and Wildlife Foundation, Project 94-237, Kodiak, Alaska.

112a. Barnes, V. G., Jr., and R. B. Smith. 1991. Survival and productivity of female brown bears on Kodiak Island, Alaska. Progress Report to the Kodiak Brown Bear Restoration and Habitat Maintenance Trust, Kodiak, Alaska.

112b. Smith, R. B., and L. J. Van Daele. 1990. Impacts of hydroelectric development on brown bears, Kodiak Island, Alaska. pp. 93–103. Proceedings of International Conference on Bear Research and Management.

113. Smith, R. B. 1989. Unit 8 deer survey-inventory progress report. in Morgan, S. O., editor. Annual report of survey-inventory activities, Part VI. Deer. Alaska Department of Fish and Game, Juneau, Alaska. (Federal Aid in Wildlife Restoration Project, W-12-1, Study 2.0; pp. 78–112).

114. Medred, C. 1987. "The dinner bell sounds." *Anchorage Daily News.* September 29, 1987. p. E-1.

115. Smith, R. B., V. G. Barnes, Jr., and L. J. Van Daele. 1989. Brown bear-human conflicts in the Kodiak archipelago, Alaska. pp. 111–119 in Bromley, M., editor. Proceedings of a Symposium on Bear-People Conflicts; Northwest Territories, Canada.

116. Barnes, V. G., Jr. 1994. Brown bear-human interactions associated with deer hunting on Kodiak Island. 63-73. Proceedings of International Conference on Bear Research and Management.

117. Miller, S. D., G. C. White, R. A. Sellers, H. V. Reynolds, J. W. Schoen, K. Titus, V. G. Barnes, Jr., R. B. Smith, R. R. Nelson, W. B. Ballard, 1997. Brown and black bear density estimation in Alaska using radiotelemetry and replicated mark-resight techniques. Alaska Department of Fish and Game, Juneau, Alaska. (Wildlife Monograph Number 133; pp. 1–55).

118a. Barnes, V.G., Jr. and R.B.Smith. 1998. Estimates of brown bear abundance on Kodiak Island, Alaska. *Ursus* 10:1–9.

118b. Barnes, V. G., Jr., R. B. Smith, and L.J. Van Daele. 1988. Density estimates and estimated population of brown bears on Kodiak and adjacent islands, 1987. Report prepared for the Kodiak Brown Bear Restoration and Habitat Maintenance Trust, Kodiak, Alaska.

119. Barnes, V.G., Jr. and R.B.Smith. 1998. Estimates of brown bear abundance on Kodiak Island, Alaska. *Ursus* 10:1–9.

120. Brown, T. 1970. Miller wants federal probe on spill. *Anchorage Daily News*. March 2, 1970. pp. 1, 2, and 6.

121. Richardson, T., and D. Cline. 2000. *Kodiak Bears and the Exxon Valdez—A Conservation Saga in Alaska's Kodiak Archepelago*. Kodiak Brown Bear Trust. Anchorgae, Alaska. 170 pgs.

122. Matt, C., B. Bartley, T. DeBruyn, D. Galla, M. McDonald, S. Mills, J. Neary, D. Shideler, and L. J. Van Daele. 2000. Bear/human conflict workshop recommendations and summary. Alaska Department of Fish and Game, Alaska Interagency Bear Safety Education Committee, Anchorage, Alaska.

123. *Exxon Valdez* Oil Spill Trustee Council. 2000. *Exxon Valdez* oil spill restoration 10-year report. Accessed November 6, 2000. <http://www.oilspill.state.ak.us>.

124. *Exxon Valdez* Oil Spill Trustee Council. 2000. *Exxon Valdez* oil spill restoration 10-year report. Accessed November 6, 2000. <http://www.oilspill.state.ak.us>.

125. Sellers, R. A., and S. D. Miller. 2000. Brown bear population dynamics in Alaska after the Exxon Valdez oil spill. *Ursus*. 12:(in press).

126. Richardson, T., and D. Cline. 2000. *Kodiak Bears and the Exxon Valdez—A Conservation Saga in Alaska's Kodiak Archepelago*. Kodiak Brown Bear Trust. Anchorgae, Alaska. 170 pgs.

127. Richardson, T., and D. Cline. 2000. *Kodiak Bears and the Exxon Valdez—A Conservation Saga in Alaska's Kodiak Archepelago*. Kodiak Brown Bear Trust. Anchorgae, Alaska. 170 pgs.

128. Kodiak Brown Bear Trust. 1996. Kodiak Brown Bear Trust—1996 Annual Report. Kodiak Brown Bear Trust, Anchorage, Alaska.

129. Van Daele, L. J. 1999. Brown bear management report—Game Management Unit 8; annual report of survey-inventory activities. Alaska Department of Fish and Game, Juneau, Alaska. (Federal Aid in Wildlife Restoration Project; in press).

130. Van Daele, L.J. 1999. 2000. The 1999 Bear Chronicles. *Kodiak Daily Mirror*. April 4, 2000. (16-page supplement).

131. Van Daele, L. J. 1999. Brown bear management report—Game Management Unit 8; annual report of survey-inventory activities. Alaska Department of Fish and Game, Juneau, Alaska. (Federal Aid in Wildlife Restoration Project; in press).

132. KNWR. 1987. Kodiak National Wildlife Refuge Comprehensive Conservation Plan, Environmental Impact Statement, and Wilderness Review. U.S. Fish and Wildlife Service, Anchorage, Alaska

133. KNWR. 1993. Public Use Management Plan and Environmental Assessment for Public Use Regulations. U.S. Fish and Wildlife Service, Kodiak, Alaska.

134. Smith, R. B. 1995. Unit 8 brown bear management report of survey-inventory activities. Alaska Department of Fish and Game, Juneau, Alaska. (Federal Aid in Wildlife Restoration Project; W-24-1 and W-24-2, Study 4.0; pp. 78–112).

135. Wilker, G. A., and V. G. Barnes, Jr. 1998. Responses of brown bears to human activities at O'Malley River, Kodiak Island, Alaska. *Ursus* 10:557–561.

136. Van Daele, L.J. 1999. 2000. The 1999 Bear Chronicles. *Kodiak Daily Mirror*. April 4, 2000. (16-page supplement).

137. Alaska Department of Fish and Game. 2002. Kodiak Archipelago Bear Conservation and Management Plan. Alaska Department of Fish and Game, Anchorage, Alaska.

"*The History Of Bears On The Kodiak Archipelago* is a splendidly researched, well balanced and instructive treatise on one of the world's most magnificent creatures. Biologist Larry Van Daele gives the reader a well-guided tour of the middle ground between the extreme swings of the pendulum — which on, one side contends 'the only good bear is a dead bear' and the other which ennobles the beast beyond recognition. For those who prefer facts, I highly recommend it."

-- *Gov. Jay Hammond*

Alaska
Natural History
A S S O C I A T I O N

Alaska Natural History Association's Mission:
An informed public caring for Alaska's natural and cultural heritage.

It is the mission of the Alaska Department of Fish and Game, Division of Wildlife Conservation, to conserve and enhance Alaska's wildife and to provide for a wide range of uses for the greastest benefit of current and future generations.